ESSENTIALS OF

Descriptive-Interpretive
Qualitative Research

Essentials of Qualitative Methods Series

ESSENTIALS OF

Descriptive-Interpretive Qualitative Research

A Generic Approach

Robert Elliott

Ladislav Timulak

 AMERICAN PSYCHOLOGICAL ASSOCIATION

Copyright © 2021 by the American Psychological Association. All rights reserved. Except as permitted under the United States Copyright Act of 1976, no part of this publication may be reproduced or distributed in any form or by any means, including, but not limited to, the process of scanning and digitization, or stored in a database or retrieval system, without the prior written permission of the publisher.

The opinions and statements published are the responsibility of the authors, and such opinions and statements do not necessarily represent the policies of the American Psychological Association.

Published by
American Psychological Association
750 First Street, NE
Washington, DC 20002
https://www.apa.org

Order Department
https://www.apa.org/pubs/books
order@apa.org

In the U.K., Europe, Africa, and the Middle East, copies may be ordered from Eurospan
https://www.eurospanbookstore.com/apa
info@eurospangroup.com

Typeset in Charter and Interstate by Circle Graphics, Inc., Reisterstown, MD

Printer: Gasch Printing, Odenton, MD
Cover Designer: Anne C. Kerns, Anne Likes Red, Inc., Silver Spring, MD

Library of Congress Cataloging-in-Publication Data

Names: Elliott, Robert (Psychologist) author. | Timulak, Ladislav, author.
Title: Essentials of descriptive-interpretive qualitative research :
  a generic approach / by Robert Elliott and Ladislav Timulak.
Description: Washington : American Psychological Association, 2021. |
  Series: Essentials of qualitative methods | Includes bibliographical
  references and index.
Identifiers: LCCN 2020030302 (print) | LCCN 2020030303 (ebook) |
  ISBN 9781433833717 (paperback) | ISBN 9781433834806 (ebook)
Subjects: LCSH: Psychology—Research—Methodology. | Qualitative research.
Classification: LCC BF76.5 .E435 2021 (print) | LCC BF76.5 (ebook) |
  DDC 150.72/3—dc23
LC record available at https://lccn.loc.gov/2020030302
LC ebook record available at https://lccn.loc.gov/2020030303

https://doi.org/10.1037/0000224-000

Printed in the United States of America

10 9 8 7 6 5 4 3 2

Contents

Series Foreword

Qualitative approaches have become accepted and indeed embraced as empirical methods within the social sciences, as scholars have realized that many of the phenomena in which we are interested are complex and require deep inner reflection and equally penetrating examination. Quantitative approaches often cannot capture such phenomena well through their standard methods (e.g., self-report measures), so qualitative designs using interviews and other in-depth data-gathering procedures offer exciting, nimble, and useful research approaches.

Indeed, the number and variety of qualitative approaches that have been developed is remarkable. We remember Bill Stiles saying (quoting Chairman Mao) at one meeting about methods, "Let a hundred flowers bloom," indicating that there are many appropriate methods for addressing research questions. In this series, we celebrate this diversity (hence, the cover design of flowers).

The question for many of us, though, has been how to decide among approaches and how to learn the different methods. Many prior descriptions of the various qualitative methods have not provided clear enough descriptions of the methods, making it difficult for novice researchers to learn how to use them. Thus, those interested in learning about and pursuing qualitative research need crisp and thorough descriptions of these approaches, with lots of examples to illustrate the method so that readers can grasp how to use the methods.

The purpose of this series of books, then, is to present a range of different qualitative approaches that seemed most exciting and illustrative of the range of methods appropriate for social science research. We asked leading experts in qualitative methods to contribute to the series, and we were delighted that they accepted our invitation. Through this series, readers have the opportunity to learn qualitative research methods from those who developed the methods and/or who have been using them successfully for years.

We asked the authors of each book to provide context for the method, including a rationale, situating the method within the qualitative tradition, describing the method's philosophical and epistemological background, and noting the key features of the method. We then asked them to describe in detail the steps of the method, including the research team, sampling, biases and expectations, data collection, data analysis, and variations on the method. We also asked authors to provide tips for the research process and for writing a manuscript emerging from a study that used the method. Finally, we asked authors to reflect on the methodological integrity of the approach, along with the benefits and limitations of the particular method.

This series of books can be used in several different ways. Instructors teaching courses in qualitative research could use the whole series, presenting one method at a time as they expose students to a range of qualitative methods. Alternatively, instructors could choose to focus on just a few approaches, as depicted in specific books, supplementing the books with examples from studies that have been published using the approaches, and providing experiential exercises to help students get started using the approaches.

In this particular book, we present Robert Elliott and Ladislav Timulak's descriptive-interpretive qualitative research methods. This generic approach is the culmination of many years of method development and research by these authors, who were pioneers in introducing qualitative research to the psychotherapy field. The main feature of this book is the integration of methods from across qualitative traditions, particularly grounded theory approaches, with an emphasis on carefully thinking through each decision. Descriptive-interpretive qualitative research is especially rich in analyzing data at both the descriptive (surface) and interpretive (deeper) levels and telling a coherent story that weaves in historical context and theory. The authors also offer a wealth of suggestions, based on their experience, about how to avoid potential methodological pitfalls.

—*Clara E. Hill and Sarah Knox*

ESSENTIALS OF

Descriptive-Interpretive Qualitative Research

1 WHY A GENERIC APPROACH TO DESCRIPTIVE-INTERPRETIVE QUALITATIVE RESEARCH?

The approach to qualitative research we present here is based on our experience and represents our values. In the first place, we take a pragmatic attitude toward research. Like you, we find ourselves embedded in a rich, complex, often confusing world, and we want to do our best to understand it in the time we have. For us, like Feyerabend (1975) in *Against Method*, science is about accomplishing practical tasks of understanding the world and ourselves in that world. Methods, theories about method (i.e., methodologies), and rules or guidelines for using those methods are all tools to help us do research carefully and effectively and solve problems we encounter in research. As researchers, we need creativity and flexibility to enhance the accuracy and usefulness of our research. This means that sometimes old established rules have to be broken, rules such as requiring research to be based only on direct observation, produce results in the form of numbers, and test theories. Knowing which rules to break and when is the hard part, but the result is a kind of grounded, creative freedom in which new research methods can emerge, guided by new sets of rules or guidelines.

https://doi.org/10.1037/0000224-001
Essentials of Descriptive-Interpretive Qualitative Research: A Generic Approach,
by R. Elliott and L. Timulak
Copyright © 2021 by the American Psychological Association. All rights reserved.

These, in turn, will later be adapted or even broken and replaced by further developments. This vision of research method as a constant process of creative flux in a dialectic of constraint and freedom, structure and chaos, has guided our careers as researchers and, particularly, as practitioners of qualitative research.

Throughout this book, you will see this stance in our approach to qualitative research. You will see it reflected in the methodological pluralism of our approach, in our support of a range of different styles of doing qualitative research carried out by different researchers tackling different topics and research problems. At the same time, you will also see that we are not, by any means, advocating an anything-goes approach to qualitative research. Instead, we try to provide a practical, no-nonsense approach centered on what we see as the essential core of many of the key forms of qualitative research being practiced today. We also point to some of the different useful options than can be added to this core, the research equivalent of a musical theme with variations.

QUALITATIVE RESEARCH AS A DESCRIPTIVE-INTERPRETIVE PROCESS

Our central argument, proposed in Elliott and Timulak (2005) and spelled out in greater detail here, is that a range of widely practiced qualitative methods with different names are, in essence, variations on a common core of a highly similar set of strategies and procedures, which we collectively refer to as *descriptive-interpretive* (or in the United Kingdom and Ireland, *interpretative*). In this, we follow both McLeod (2011), who grouped most of these approaches under the headings of grounded theory and "variants of grounded theory" (p. 144), and Rennie (2012), who characterized them as centrally involving both description and interpretation. Rennie referred to these approaches as "hermeneutic" (which is just a fancy word for "interpretive"), writing that they represented the difficult middle path between realism and relativism (Rennie, 1998). This family of qualitative methods includes grounded theory (Charmaz, 2006; Glaser & Strauss, 1967; Rennie et al., 1988), consensual qualitative research (Hill, 2012; Hill et al., 1997), empirical phenomenology (Giorgi, 1975; Wertz, 1983), hermeneutic-interpretive research (Packer & Addison, 1989), interpretative phenomenological analysis (Smith et al., 2009), thematic analysis (Braun & Clarke, 2006), and so on.

In our view, these approaches, which we refer to as *generic descriptive-interpretive qualitative research* (GDI-QR), all involve the following:

- posing open-ended, exploratory research questions, which then guide the study and begin to define domains of investigation;
- collecting open-ended (nonnumerical) verbally reported experiences or observations to answer these research questions;
- committing to the careful, systematic analysis of all relevant reports and observations;
- coming to a descriptive-interpretive understanding of experiences and observations by carefully representing their meaning;
- organizing these understandings into clusters of similar experiences and observations (categories, themes, codes, etc.);
- being critically aware of and disclosing the researcher's interests (domains of investigation), prior expectations, and organizing conceptual framework (theory) as these have helped understand and organize experiences, observations, and categories; and
- integrating categories into some kind of coherent story or model.

For example, in regard to the third point, some of these approaches initiate the process of data analysis by looking at the data line-by-line and writing initial notes (variously referred to as "codes," "provisional categories," "provisional themes") on the margin of the document, whereas other approaches first break the text into paragraphs or sentences (also referred to as "meaning units") before starting to write notes (e.g., codes, provisional categories, provisional themes). Nevertheless, although referred to differently in the different brand-named methods, all of this essentially involves dividing text into manageable chunks, then translating and illuminating the meaning conveyed. Similarly, overlap in the strategies used is visible in other steps of the data analysis process, as we elaborate in Chapter 4.

ORIGINS OF THIS APPROACH TO QUALITATIVE RESEARCH

Before going further, however, we are going to tell you a bit about ourselves. We (Robert and Ladislav—Laco, for short, pronounced "Latso") are both qualitative researchers by inclination and preference but psychotherapy researchers beyond that. We have experience applying a broad array of methods (including randomized controlled trials). We are also both practicing therapists coming from a humanistic-experiential theoretical orientation— more specifically, emotion-focused therapy. We thus see ourselves as psychotherapy researchers first and foremost but feel most happy doing qualitative research. In our experience, research and biography are deeply interwoven for us, so we think it is useful to lay out in more detail who we are and how we got to the position we are taking in this book.

Robert's Story

I (Robert) struggled with numbers as a little boy but fell in love with taxonomic systems in biology when I was 10 years old; I have been classifying things ever since. In graduate school, my comprehensive exam essay was a qualitative meta-analysis of the literature of descriptions of therapist in-session intentions (Elliott, 1977), and I did a minor in conversation analysis, studying with Manny Schegloff (Sacks et al., 1974). In 1976, in the process of randomly sampling short segments of therapy sessions, I accidentally came across my first significant therapy event (Elliott, 1983) and set about developing research methods for analyzing these key moments of therapeutic change. At first, I tried applying quantitative methods to do this (e.g., Elliott, 1984); however, I soon became frustrated with these and, over the course of the 1980s, increasingly moved toward qualitative methods— in particular, grounded theory analysis, following the Rennie interpretation (Rennie et al., 1988), with an infusion of empirical phenomenology, following the Wertz (1983) interpretation. Eventually, I developed comprehensive process analysis, a complex descriptive-interpretive approach for analyzing significant therapy events (Elliott et al., 1994).

Having embraced qualitative research by around 1985, I then spent the next 15 years of my career as a qualitative researcher engaged in activities aimed at establishing and legitimizing qualitative research: reading philosophy of science (e.g., Polkinghorne, 1983), developing a critique of conventional quantitative psychotherapy research (e.g., Elliott & Anderson, 1994), and developing and trying to publish systematic guidelines for qualitative research. Thus, in the latter part of the 1990s, I collaborated with Connie Fischer and David Rennie to develop a set of guidelines for designing and evaluating qualitative research studies (Elliott et al., 1999).

My early published qualitative research (e.g., Elliott et al., 1994) contained numerous attempts to apply quantitative-appearing procedures to qualitative research, including auditing methods (to parallel interrater reliability), systematic assessment of researcher expectations, and quantification of qualitative themes across participants to facilitate interpretation of findings (e.g., general vs. variant categories), elements that were later incorporated into consensual qualitative research (Hill et al., 1997; Rhodes et al., 1994). I subsequently concluded that the specific details of this legitimization project went beyond what is necessary and became worried that restricting qualitative research practice to these particular practices could curtail the creativity and flexibility needed for qualitative research to thrive. I have spent the past 20 years happily skating among a wide range of qualitative and quantitative approaches but always find myself returning to the descriptive-interpretive approach we describe here; it is the place where I feel most myself as a researcher.

Laco's Story

I (Laco) am of a younger generation of qualitative psychotherapy researchers (although nearing my 50s now). Inspired by Robert's work, as well as by the work of other first-generation qualitative psychotherapy researchers such as David Rennie, Bill Stiles, John McLeod, and Clara Hill, I developed my approach to conducting qualitative psychotherapy research as a result of seeking to understand (from reading published qualitative papers) how these researchers (and other colleagues) went about conducting qualitative research. Then, in the early 2000s, during a Fulbright Fellowship, I had an opportunity to collaborate with Robert and learn firsthand about Robert's experiences of conducting qualitative research. This was reassuring because it further confirmed that what I was doing (in my own (on the basis of reading the writing of the aforementioned researchers) was similar to how Robert worked. The two of us then presented the basic features of how we do qualitative research in a chapter for a book on research methods in clinical and health psychology (Elliott & Timulak, 2005); this allowed us to begin to outline the approach to qualitative research presented in this book.

QUALITATIVE RESEARCH AND THE BRAND NAMES PROBLEM

The most striking aspect of the current state of qualitative research is just how many different brands of qualitative research there are, all seeking recognition and place. In our experience, newcomers find this quite intimidating. We look at our students and imagine them wondering why qualitative research cannot be more like quantitative research, which appears (at least if you do not look too closely) to have a much more defined set of analytic procedures, such as means, standard deviations, tests of differences (*t*-tests and effect sizes), and tests of association (correlations). We find ourselves apologizing for the situation and making excuses—for example, explaining that it is because modern qualitative research is so new and has not had time to consolidate yet into a unified shared consensus. However, we do empathize with their struggle in the face of the range of approaches.

As an illustration of the distortions that can emerge from the present situation, one of us (Laco) once had the experience of assessing two sets of student research projects for a university course. Students had been encouraged to produce two research projects using different methods over the course of their studies. However, Laco found multiple instances in which both projects were qualitative and were similar in the procedures used and the presentation of findings, although students had clearly followed, as instructed, two different brand-named qualitative methods.

Conversely, studies claiming to follow the same method may diverge in their procedures due to a variety of factors, including the phenomenon studied and the scientific discipline the study was embedded in, or simply due to differences in training, individual researchers' practice, or the traditions of the institutions in which the researchers worked. It is thus quite difficult to distinguish clear boundaries between what constitutes one brand-name method and what distinguishes it from another. Indeed, we are not the only ones to notice this: A qualitative meta-method study of 109 qualitative studies of clients' experiences of therapy conducted by Levitt, Pomerville, and colleagues (2017) showed that studies that were supposedly following the same brand-name approach (e.g., grounded theory) did not necessarily follow the same strategies and procedures and could potentially share more in common with studies using a different brand-name approach (e.g., interpretative phenomenological analysis) than with each other. As with brands of psychotherapy, labeling studies with different brand names thus does not guarantee that different methodological strategies and procedures have been used. By the same token, applying the same brand-name methodological approach to two studies by no means guarantees similarity of strategies and procedures. Therefore, we talk about "generic" or "descriptive-interpretive" approaches to qualitative research that share in common an effort to describe, summarize, and classify what is present in the data, which always, as we explain in Chapter 4, involves a degree of interpretation.

The emergence of a wide range of highly similar but differently branded qualitative research approaches is perfectly understandable and worth considering here. Despite our position in favor of a generic descriptive-interpretive approach to qualitative research, we recognize that there are some inherent benefits to the use of brand-name approaches. Editors, reviewers, and often also readers expect to see specific methods referred to in manuscripts because this is how the scholarly community functions. When we come up with a methodological procedure, we name and thus brand it. This gives recognition to the founder of the method, but it is also a clear reference point for the scholarly community. Later researchers can then follow a procedure as presented in methodological publications. Branding gives a sense of solidity or grounding to qualitative researchers and readers. Indeed, if authors do not cite or follow an established brand-name method, they may be questioned in the review process regarding what method of qualitative research they used. This has happened to us often enough that Laco (inspired by his students) started to use the term "descriptive-interpretive" as if it was a brand name, in the process citing our chapter from 2005 as the so-called manual of the method.

The use of a specific brand-named procedure, as described in a brand-named manual, can thus be understood as bringing some sense of safety and increasing the likelihood that the research will be respected by the community. The unintended consequence here is that the work may start to be scrutinized as to whether it fits the original description. (One of us was once criticized by a reviewer for not following the procedure as outlined in the original description of the "method," despite being both the author of the description of the method and the criticized, nonmethod-following person). More important, following a manualized brand-named method in an unreflective step-by-step manner brings a potential constraint to the creativity of qualitative research. It inflates the weight of a specific procedure that is potentially one of infinite variations of similar methods. This is why we feel passionate about the usefulness of a generic approach that allows qualitative researchers to adapt sets of strategies and procedures that fit their analytic style as researchers, the topic under investigation, and the nature of the data collected.

Obviously, we are not alone in our perspective. For instance, John McLeod (2001, 2011), a Scottish qualitative psychotherapy researcher, following Denzin and Lincoln (1994), likened qualitative psychotherapy researchers to *bricoleurs*, a French word for people who carry out do-it-yourself activities "using whatever materials are available" (Baldick, 2008, p. 42). This makes qualitative research a form of *bricolage* (something constructed by bricoleurs), adapted to make use of the available means to address the research problem or question at hand. Of course, the bricolage still has to hang together in a coherent, logical fashion and be consistent with our underlying principles and standards (see Chapter 6).

WHAT LIES OUTSIDE THE DESCRIPTIVE-INTERPRETIVE GENRE OF QUALITATIVE RESEARCH?

Although we talk about a generic approach to qualitative research, we delineate a boundary between those qualitative approaches that we do and do not include in our thinking. Approaches we see as not so comfortably fitting within the GDI-QR paradigm include approaches referred to by Ponterotto (2005) as belonging to a critical-ideological paradigm (e.g., feminist approaches) and also approaches that study language and communication (e.g., discourse analysis and conversation analysis). Along with autoethnography (Etherington, 2004), these approaches have their own solid traditions and distinct rules of investigation forming a particular discipline. These approaches adopt a particular researcher stance that analyzes data from a particular discipline-specific or philosophical perspective. On the one hand, critical ideological research (e.g., Lather, 1991) privileges a particular liberating theory (e.g., feminist) as central and then uses findings to illustrate the theory, making it theory-centered to a far greater extent than descriptive-interpretive research is. On the other hand, discourse analysis is much closer to linguistics in its focus (on general cultural practices rather on personal experience) and methods (e.g., proof by example, searching for exceptions).

We do acknowledge possible overlapping elements between GDI-QR and critical-ideological approaches or discourse analysis approaches; however, descriptive-interpretive approaches are usually based on learning from participants in a way that allows the interpretive lenses to be somewhat looser or informed and altered by the phenomenon under investigation. That does not mean that the generic method cannot be theory informed (Hissa & Timulak, 2020; Stiles, 2003; Timulak & Elliott, 2019). In this case, however, theory is not there to illuminate the phenomenon (as in critical-ideological research), nor is the kind of theory focused on broader cultural resources and practices (as opposed to personal experiences and psychological phenomena or processes). Instead, the theory is there to prioritize and shape but, more important, to be built (as in Stiles's 2015 theory-building research)—that is, to be further nuanced, altered, or challenged by the observed data. Often, the theory is tacit, present in the researchers' background and position, and the data help bring out the researchers' implicit theory.

PSYCHOTHERAPY AND PSYCHOTHERAPY RESEARCH AS CONTEXT FOR OUR APPROACH

We believe more broadly that the discipline within which various qualitative studies are conducted does shape those studies (Timulak & Elliott, 2019), and thus, awareness of this should be a part of the qualitative method used in the study. We illustrate using our discipline (psychotherapy research) what we mean by our claim that the context of one's discipline is part of the method, which grounds and shapes how the study is conducted and presented. As noted earlier, Robert has been involved with qualitative psychotherapy research for over 40 years, Laco for about 25. Between the two of us, we have conducted or supervised perhaps more than 200 qualitative studies. We have served as reviewers on various journals, served on the editorial boards of several journals, and have been editors of journals publishing qualitative psychotherapy research. We have conducted or have been involved in studies that used interviews, focus groups, observations, think-aloud protocols, tape-assisted recalls, questionnaires, retrospective recalls, and so forth. We have been involved in studies or reviewed studies that we include among the brand-named approaches that we see as covered by our broader definition of generic, descriptive, and interpretive research. The fact that we are psychotherapists and psychotherapy researchers has not only shaped who we are but has also deeply affected our work as qualitative researchers.

Specifically, we understand psychotherapy as a practice that involves the therapist inquiring into the client's experience. This activity is quite similar to the activity of qualitative researchers who, when collecting data, often immerse themselves in the experiences of their participants. This similarity between the process of therapy and the process of qualitative research (as well as the relevance of participant experience to both therapy and research about therapy) may explain the relatively early popularity of qualitative methods among psychotherapy and counseling researchers.

Qualitative research in the study of psychotherapy has also been influenced by the place psychotherapy and its scholarly tradition and practical applications has in society. For instance, phenomena relevant to psychotherapy are potential topics for qualitative investigations (e.g., clients' experiences of various aspects of therapy or their difficulties, therapists' experiences of various aspects of delivering therapy, the therapeutic relationship, transference, countertransference, emotional transformation, therapists' experiences of training). In terms of how we want to study these questions, we may rely at times on the client perspective and at other times on the therapist perspective, or we may have to focus on the observation of therapy recordings or even the perspective of people in the clients' broader social circle, and so forth. Qualitative research on all these aspects of psychotherapy provides a fuller, richer understanding of the nature of psychotherapy and how it can be improved.

The discipline context influences what qualitative methods are regarded as acceptable, relevant, and credible by a broader audience who may include practitioners, psychotherapy trainers, psychotherapy supervisors, and psychotherapy scholars, as well as other stakeholders such as clients, relatives, or representatives of the broader community that avails itself of psychotherapy services or who may be in charge of funding those services. Qualitative psychotherapy studies are thus influenced by developments in psychotherapy and related disciplines, such as applied clinical and counseling psychology, and by developments in broader psychotherapy research and research in related disciplines.

PHILOSOPHICAL AND EPISTEMOLOGICAL BACKGROUND

To situate ourselves explicitly for the reader in relation to what follows, we offer the following description of our epistemological stance (see also Timulak & Elliott, 2019). We see ourselves as broadly embracing a position that can be described as critical realism (Barker et al., 2015; Elliott & Anderson, 1994) and dialectical constructivism (Elliott & Greenberg, 1997; Pascual-Leone, 1991).

Critical Realism

Critical realism evolved in the latter half of the 20th century, moving beyond earlier realist or positivist positions (Bhaskar, 1978) that had dominated behaviorist psychology. These earlier positions had emphasized a *correspondence theory* of truth, which asserts that a theory or description of the world is true if it matches reality. A *critical realist* position (Cook & Campbell, 1979) assumes that there exists a real world out there, which can be at least partially known and against which we can check our findings and theories but which, at the same time, can never be known with certainty; all our understandings are essentially tentative and limited by the perspective from which they are offered. Because of the limits of all methods, multiple perspectives, observers, and even (especially!) research designs are needed for coming to truly understand a topic, such as how change occurs in psychotherapy or people's lives.

The critical realist position thus emphasizes various kinds of replication: by other methods, other researchers, application to new populations, and so forth. In the realm of qualitative research this means that knowledge should be intersubjectively testable (Cook & Campbell, 1979; Popper, 1959); that is, other researchers should be able to replicate the study by arriving at findings that we can recognize as similar or at least complementary (because no two qualitative researchers will analyze a set of data in the same way). Beyond this, critical realism suggests that qualitative researchers should, over time, approach the same topic using different methods with complementary strengths and weaknesses, a strategy often referred to as "triangulation" (Tashakkori & Teddlie, 2009). Thus, in terms of truth criteria (Packer & Addison, 1989), critical realism goes beyond correspondence theory to include consensus theory (i.e., truth by agreement among different researchers) and coherence theory (converging observations should be consistent with one another).

Dialectical Constructivism

At the same time, we argue that our approach is also a form of *dialectical constructivism* (Greenberg & Pascual-Leone, 1995; Pascual-Leone, 1991), a philosophical position that sees knowers (e.g., qualitative researchers) not as detached observers but as actively interacting with what they are trying to know. Thus, the collection, analysis, and interpretation of qualitative data all involve processes of interactive construction. In the case of data collection, the dialectic is a literal dialog between researcher and participant (or therapist and client when therapy session transcripts are used as data). In data analysis, the researcher enters into a metaphorical "dialog with the data" by asking questions of their meaning units and then looking for answers in their analysis; in the writing stage the qualitative researcher acts as a mediator (*inter + preter*—i.e., one who speaks between) between the data and the reader. Dialectical constructivism (which, incidentally, is also the philosophical basis of emotion-focused therapy) holds that coming to know something changes both the state of our knowledge and the something itself (see also Piaget, 1970; Vygotsky, 1978). This means that the process of interviewing an interviewee about their experience of gender fluidity is likely to change both the way the researcher understands gender and the interviewee's gender identity.

If the main practical implications of critical realism are replication and triangulation, the main practical implications of dialectical constructivism are the importance of specifying the researcher's prior understandings or theory and treating qualitative research as dialogue.

A FEW KEY POINTERS FOR READERS

In the following pages, we describe our suggestions and tips for conducting a broad range of qualitative investigations that come under the umbrella of GDI-QR. We conclude this chapter with two key pointers about our presentation.

First, we use terms such as "domains," "meaning units," "categories," and so forth, that may be used similarly or differently by various brand-named methods or approaches. We do not insist on using those terms in the way we are using them here. The use of the same terminology is not defining of the "method" we are describing here. What is defining is the spirit or general idea and the picture of how to go about designing a study that fits the researchers' research question.

Second, the examples we use most often come from psychotherapy because this is the discipline with which we are most familiar. Many examples will be from studies we have carried out or supervised; they, therefore, illustrate the problems with which we have had to grapple. We certainly do not think that the application of GDI-QR is limited to psychotherapy research, but we recognize that some readers may have to use their imagination to extend these examples to their disciplines or topics.

2 DESIGNING THE STUDY

In this chapter, we address the preliminary or planning phase of generic descriptive-interpretive qualitative research (GDI-QR). This is the part of the research process where you define your research topic and questions, recruit folks for the research team, decide what kind of data you are going to collect and who the participants will be and how you will recruit them, explicate your expectations and guiding conceptual framework, and design the integrity checks you are going build in to enhance the persuasiveness of your study. Because qualitative research in general, and GDI-QR in particular, is more flexible than traditional quantitative research, it is more difficult to maintain neat distinctions between planning, data collection, and data analysis, which means that the placement of material in this and the next two chapters is somewhat arbitrary and will require a certain amount of cross-referencing.

https://doi.org/10.1037/0000224-002

Essentials of Descriptive-Interpretive Qualitative Research: A Generic Approach, by R. Elliott and L. Timulak
Copyright © 2021 by the American Psychological Association. All rights reserved.

DEFINING THE RESEARCH PROBLEM AND QUESTIONS

Two key points about designing GDI-QR studies have emerged from our long experience doing qualitative research. First, a clear definition of the topic, together with a clear statement of the research questions, is the most important requirement of a good qualitative study. In fact, we see this as more important than the specific method used. A poorly defined topic and badly worded set of research questions will haunt a qualitative study all its days, damaging its credibility and usability and making everyone miserable along the way. Therefore, it is vitally important for researchers to invest time in carefully thinking about and discussing their topic and what research questions are most interesting and relevant at the moment. What do we know so far? What is the next logical question to ask?

Second, qualitative research is really good in general for answering open, exploratory research questions, such as "How do people experience wearing a nicotine patch in the early phase of trying to stop smoking?" Such research questions are sometimes referred to as "discovery oriented" because they seek to uncover the range and varieties of a particular phenomenon (kind of experience or observable action), including its sources and how it unfolds over time; in essence, they seek to map out the territory for later research. Conversely, if the main research questions are closed—if they seek to test or confirm our theory, hypotheses, or hopes—a qualitative study may not be the best choice. If you want to prove that your favorite kind of therapy works, you are generally better off doing a quantitative outcome study because it will be easier to do and more effective in answering your research question.

Types of Qualitative Research Questions

We see GDI-QR as applicable to a broad range of research questions. However, if we were to characterize the typical research questions investigated using the procedures articulated in this book, they would share the following features: They generally include open-ended, exploratory questions and seek to address complex issues (cf. Barker et al., 2015), such as "How do clients experience the therapy hour moment by moment?" (Rennie, 1990), "What kinds of significant therapy events are there?" (Elliott, 1985), and "What kinds of experiences do family therapists report during individual therapy sessions?" (Rober et al., 2008). These are qualitative psychotherapy research questions; similar questions can be found in any social, human, or health science field. Typically, we want to learn about a phenomenon in great detail, not simply answering "yes" or "no" but instead unfolding the nuances to get a rich sense of the texture of what we are studying.

If you want to stimulate your creativity, try using the following framework of three types of research questions that lend themselves to GDI-QR (Elliott, 1995):

- *Definitional* questions ask about the nature or essence of some phenomenon, that is, what makes it what it is and not something else—for example, "What are the essential aspects that define the experience of being criminally victimized?" (Wertz, 1985). Such questions have been emphasized by empirical phenomenology (Giorgi, 1975; Wertz, 1983).

- *Descriptive* research questions seek answers about features, types, or patterns within a phenomenon. In particular, they ask about the existence and diversity of particular experiences or observations—for example, "How do gay or queer men who perform in drag experience gender?" (Levitt, Surace, et al., 2018).

- *Explanatory* questions seek in-depth understandings of how things come about or unfold. For example, the researcher may be faced with a puzzling or interesting event, such as instances in which a therapist misunderstands a client or in which a person is able to quit drinking on their own without professional help. Here, the researcher wants to come to an understanding of the various factors that may have brought this event about. Hermeneutic brands of GDI-QR (e.g., Packer & Addison, 1989) and comprehensive process analysis (Elliott et al., 1994) have emphasized this sort of research question. The idea here is to create an understanding or even a tentative model of how something may have come about.

Engaging With the Literature

We certainly do not subscribe to the view put forward by Glaser (1978) that you should not read the relevant literature to avoid biasing yourself. Instead, we assert that it is valuable for qualitative studies to be anchored in a thorough scholarly engagement with the literature. Reading the relevant literature helps you develop a clear rationale for the study. It establishes what is known in the field, what has been studied, and what factors may influence findings. It helps you see whether there is a need for the study and what questions are begging to be answered, whose answers will have scientific or practical utility. In fact, it is our view that whether the research takes a quantitative or qualitative approach is secondary to answering the research questions; in other words, the fact that a study may end up as a qualitative study optimally emerges from the nature of the problem the researchers want to address (Elliott & Timulak, 2005).

Therefore, we argue for a responsible and scholarly approach to qualitative research grounded in the relevant literature. This requires disciplined reflection and critical thinking on the researcher's side throughout the research process, starting with an awareness of how particular research problems and research questions came about in the researcher's mind and how they emerge from the existing literature (Rennie, 2012). What assumptions underpin this articulation of the problem (and related questions), and in what larger perspective in the literature are those assumptions embedded? What function may these assumptions serve for the researcher? What would challenging them mean? And so forth. We encourage an attitude of self-awareness, self-scrutiny, and openness to learning—in particular, an openness to new findings that might challenge and shake preconceptions, thus changing us and our theoretical conceptualizations.

There is another reason for reading the available literature: It can help you think more clearly about your topic and research questions. In particular, a careful reading of the available theoretical and research literature can help you clarify what it is and is not, along with its likely aspects and variations. In other words, it can help you do a *conceptual analysis* of the phenomenon you want to study. This might sound a bit intimidating, but it just means trying to think logically and clearly about what you are studying and what its key aspects are. We discuss this further in Chapters 3 and 4. An example, in our case, is our background and investment in emotion-focused therapy as an important mental health intervention that informs the type of methods we prefer (e.g., focused on clients' emotional experiences), the analytical framework we adopt (e.g., examining clients' emotional experiences through the lenses of our explicit or implicit classifications of emotions), and how we present our findings (e.g., we speak to the audience of psychotherapy researchers and practitioners).

THE RESEARCH TEAM

A good qualitative researcher has to be motivated by more than fear or dislike for quantitative research. First, they have to be up for a lot of challenging, often tedious work. Second, they have to have good listening and empathic exploration or observation skills, both for collecting useful, insightful data and for understanding what their informants are trying to say about their experiences or how they behave. Third, they have to be logical, well-organized, and good with language (even poetic) to keep their analysis from descending into chaos and to create categories and summary stories that are crisp and memorable.

Although we prefer to carry out our approach to qualitative research in teams of two to four people, we do not object to using a single qualitative analyst. Rennie's (1990) highly influential and ground-breaking study of client in-session experiences is a case in point. It took him at least 10 years; he obsessively audited and reaudited his analyses, but in the end, he produced a series of reports detailed enough that readers could check his findings for themselves, findings that have radically reshaped our understanding of psychotherapy (Rennie, 1992, 1994a, 1994b, 2007). For our part, we find qualitative research to be arduous, lonely, and at times, anxiety provoking. In qualitative research, our findings are only as clear, accurate, and useful as we are able to make them. It is nice to have someone else to share the work, provide company, and rein us in if we get carried away. We find that there is safety and freedom in working with one or more coresearchers. At a minimum, we recommend working with a main researcher and an auditor to check the analyses of the main researcher.

GETTING YOUR HEAD AROUND PREUNDERSTANDINGS AND BIAS

Limitations of Bracketing

Early on, when qualitative research started to be of interest to psychology and other social science researchers, there was a naive sense that, due to its inductive nature (Glaser, 1978), the researcher should be almost a tabula rasa, approaching the phenomena of interest with no prior knowledge so as not to be biased toward the subject of study and thus to avoid influencing potential findings one way or the other. There was also a sense that qualitative research was in some essential way focused primarily on discovery (discovery-oriented research; Elliott, 1984; Mahrer, 1988) and that discovery required that researchers do not (or should not) have preconceptions. In our discipline, early qualitative studies in psychotherapy focused on the clients' experiences of therapy (e.g., Rennie, 1990), where it was seen as central that participants and clients be given a voice. Thus, the idea that researchers' biases and expectations should be bracketed (Tufford & Newman, 2012) was originally seen as a defining feature of qualitative research, especially in the phenomenological tradition and the Glaser (1978) branch of grounded theory analysis.

In contrast, consistent with Heidegger (1962) and our dialectical constructivist epistemology, we have argued elsewhere (Elliott & Timulak, 2005; Timulak & Elliott, 2019) that attempts by researchers to put aside our preconceptions are impossible to accomplish fully; there is always an interaction between what is known and what is becoming known. Our research queries and our processes of acquiring knowledge (getting to know) are both embedded in our preunderstandings. Although the bracketing metaphor is still popular in qualitative research (cf. Sim et al., 2012), it is quite clear that even when researchers try to put preconceptions aside, they do so to a questionable extent. For example, it has been demonstrated that when different research teams analyze the same data, despite efforts "to let the data speak for themselves," they come up with different findings (Ladany et al., 2012). We discuss this further in Chapters 3 and 4.

The Importance of Specifying Researcher Preunderstandings

Furthermore, not only do researchers' interpretive lenses shape their perspective on data, but their preconceptions also shape all phases of the research. Researchers' preunderstandings of the phenomenon inform their research questions and what sort of data they collect. For instance, the questions subsequently outlined in an interview schedule are, to some extent, already predetermined by the researchers' preunderstandings. Whether a psychotherapy researcher wants to see a phenomenon from the clients' perspective, the therapists' perspective, or both depends on that researcher's thinking about the phenomenon. Data may be collected in a manner informed by a concept of temporal order (e.g., what happened before deciding to stop drinking, during the process of stopping, and after stopping), or it may be informed by theory (e.g., what sort of primary and secondary emotions clients with generalized anxiety disclose in therapy sessions). Preunderstandings thus shape not only what we see in the data but also what we set out to study about the phenomenon, how we collect data, and how we structure those data (e.g., pragmatically, temporarily, theoretically).

We add here that the researchers have to be reflective of their preunderstandings, and they may also have to articulate them in advance to share them with others later. Although many qualitative research studies are silent on the role theoretical assumptions play in shaping the preunderstandings and the process of understanding the data, we urge researchers to explicitly articulate their theoretical positions starting in the planning phase of their research. Even in supposedly atheoretical studies that do not anchor themselves in an explicitly articulated theoretical framework, a mixture of personal and professional or scholarly (theoretically informed) perspectives is inevitably present when researchers collect, analyze, and interpret data.

Researchers often seek to address this by providing their background and/or expectations before the research started (cf. Hill et al., 1997, 2005; Sim et al., 2012) to situate the potential interpretive framework of the analysts for the reader. In the context of explicitly theoretically informed qualitative studies (cf. Hissa & Timulak, 2020), we recommend that there is not only a clear articulation of the interpretive framework but also of any researcher expectations, both theoretical and of a more personal nature.

Bias Exercise

Discussions of bias typically portray it as an evil that must be rooted out; therefore, we close this discussion of the need to explicate preunderstandings and biases in planning GDI-QR with one of Robert's exercises, based on the origins of the word "bias," first used in English around 1520, derived from Middle French "biais," meaning slanted, tilted, or oblique, and originally used to describe the line of the weave in fabric and other materials. Robert guides his students as follows:

> Take a piece of paper. First, fold it halfway down, so the top edge meets the bottom edge. Run your fingers down the fold, lightly creasing it. Now, unfold the paper and try folding it the other way so that the left and right edges meet. Again, run your fingers down the fold, lightly creasing it.
>
> If you haven't been too aggressive in creasing the fold, you will find that one of the folds feels bumpier than the other (usually, the first, horizontal fold). You have just experienced the bias of the paper. Bias is built into the world; it's in the basic texture of things. Everything has bias; you can't escape it.

What we are saying here is that we have to be aware of our biases, and the best time to start doing that is when you are planning your study.

CHOOSING DATA COLLECTION PROCEDURES

The generic, descriptive-interpretive approach to qualitative research that we present in this book can use a wide range of data collection procedures. Again, this should be determined by the research problem at hand and should result from the researcher's scholarly and reflective efforts to ascertain how best to collect data in a manner that might inform an understanding of the phenomenon. We, and others, have used this generic approach with qualitative interviews (e.g., Klein & Elliott, 2006; McElvaney & Timulak, 2013; Timulak et al., 2017), open-ended questionnaires (Richards & Timulak, 2012), recall-based interviews (Elliott & Shapiro, 1988; Timulak

& Elliott, 2003; Timulak & Lietaer, 2001), focus groups (e.g., Elliott et al., 2004), observations based on recordings of therapy sessions (O'Brien et al., 2019), and combinations of various data collection methods (e.g., Elliott et al., 1994; Timulak & Lietaer, 2001). All these means of collecting data have their place in qualitative research. These varied forms of data collection have in common that they primarily use verbal accounts, descriptions in words, or observations put into words (although other means, such as drawing, could also be used). Numbers are used typically only in a supportive, contextual way—for instance, in describing how representative various features of the phenomenon are of the sample. It is also possible to include quantitative ratings (e.g., a client session helpfulness rating of 9) by simply dropping the numerical value and using the verbal equivalent (e.g., *extremely helpful*) instead, a procedure that is used in comprehensive process analysis (Elliott, 1993), a mixed-methods intensive case study version of GDI-QR.

Qualitative Interviews

Interviews are probably the most common means of collecting data in qualitative research. Typically, the interviews used in qualitative research are either open ended with one broad question (e.g., "What was your experience of therapy?") or semistructured with a set of questions that are still open ended (e.g., "How did you experience your relationship with your therapist?" "How did you experience the referral process?"). Semistructured interviews use a structure that has to be clearly articulated in the planning phase of the research.

The interview schedule should typically be relatively brief, consisting of a few main open-ended questions. Participants may respond similarly to similar questions; therefore, it is advisable that researchers endeavor to avoid overlapping questions unless these are used as alternative or follow-up questions for informants who need help—for example, the main question might be "How was your day before the therapy session?" And the alternative or follow-up question might be "Can you remember how you were feeling that day before the session?" Participants will want to talk about what they want to, regardless of how nuanced interview questions are, so it may be helpful to structure the interview parsimoniously. We have experienced many (particularly student) projects that simply have too many interview questions and often may not even use open-ended questions.

Audio recording and transcribing interviews is essential in GDI-QR, and it can sometimes be a good idea to use video recording to gather data regarding participants' facial expressions, body language, or behavior during the interview. This method is used in some forms of psychoanalytic qualitative research (e.g., Brien et al., 2018). Interviews can also be conducted across several sessions, which may be particularly important if the topic is sensitive and the researchers want to develop trust and secure rapport with the participants.

There are plenty of good guides for conducting qualitative interviews (e.g., Brinkmann & Kvale, 2018; Knox & Burkard, 2009). In some cases, the participants may get an interview schedule in advance (Hill et al., 1997). The interviews can be conducted face-to-face or through the use of technology (e.g., phone, Zoom). In general, they are audio or video recorded rather than documented via note taking. Depending on the research strategy (i.e., how open ended it is), the interview schedule may also be developed across interviews, although in our experience, the interview schedule typically stays the same after initial piloting. In some cases, the interviewer may be a part of a larger research team, in some cases not. This is often a pragmatic decision that depends on the size of the research team. In any case, it is good if the interviewer is trained, has an opportunity to try out the interview, and is given feedback on the conduct of the interview.

Focus Groups

An alternative to individual qualitative interviewing is the *focus group*—an interview with a group of participants (Krueger & Casey, 2014; Stewart & Shamdasani, 2014). As with individual interviews, focus groups may be supplemented with observations documented by note taking or video recording. Focus groups can be conducted through an online environment that, in some instances, might allow more participants to be assessed and their views compared in real time. However, the number of participants in a focus group will determine how much can be covered within one session. A larger group naturally limits how much can be covered because the time devoted to accommodating all participants may limit the breadth of the questions or topics it is possible to cover.

As with individual interviews, researchers should be clear on how and for what purpose they formulated the open questions they use to stimulate discussion in the focus group. Focus groups may be particularly relevant if the researchers are also interested in social influence and consensus processes relevant to the phenomenon under investigation. For instance, if we interview young male student participants about their perceptions of help seeking in the form of counseling, we may see how some themes—for instance, whether it is manly or unmanly to seek help—play out in the group. Is there consensus or disagreement? Depending on the goal of the study, the selection of participants may vary to create a more homogenous or heterogeneous focus group. In some studies, participants in a focus group may consist of a preexisting group (e.g., a class of trainees), and such a group may have a dynamic that will have to be considered. For instance, if we interview trainees of counseling psychology programs about their experiences of training through a focus group that involves the actual class, we may expect that there may be a prior dynamic in the class that may affect whether people agree or disagree with each other.

The level of group leader moderation may also vary. To maximize potential group dynamics, the moderation of a focus group may vary in moderator directiveness, depending on the goals of the study. For instance, if we expect the topic to be controversial, it may be more interesting to have less direction so we could also observe how the group dynamic shapes itself. If, on the contrary, it is important for us to know to what extent a particular opinion is represented in the sample, we will want to ensure that all participants have a space to express their perspective. Given that interpersonal dynamics are likely to be more complex in group contexts than during individual interviews, the facilitation of focus groups may require more experience on the part of moderators. There may be participants who dominate and others who are too compliant. There may be participants who speak less because they are shy or feel they have a minority view, which they are thus less inclined to express. It is important, therefore, to be able to ensure the appropriate participation of group members. Group cohesiveness and the capability of some participants to influence other participants may also play a role (Stewart & Shamdasani, 2014). Compared with individual interviews, there are also different ethical considerations to be taken into account (e.g., regarding confidentiality among group members). There are plenty of guides for conducting focus groups that we encourage the reader to consult (e.g., Krueger & Casey, 2014; Stewart & Shamdasani, 2014).

Our qualitative research and other descriptive-interpretive approaches have only rarely used focus groups. However, in preparation for a book project, Robert once conducted a series of three focus groups of three to eight participants each to study trainee therapists' experiences of learning emotion-focused therapy (Chapter 15 of Elliott et al., 2004). The focus-group format worked well in that context because it allowed input from a relatively large number of people in a brief time and because the participants enjoyed sharing their experiences with each other, which they did enthusiastically.

Recording-Assisted Recall Interviews

Another specialized interview format, originally developed by Kagan (1975) as a counseling skill training method, is recording-assisted recall interviewing (Elliott, 1986; Elliott & Shapiro, 1988), which can be used to "get inside" an interaction process by playing recordings of the interaction back to one or more of its participants soon after it has taken place. Recording-assisted recall interviews have been used by Rennie (1992), Elliott (1986), Hill (1974), and others to study psychotherapy. This was one of the first areas in which qualitative psychotherapy research showed its potential and where it was used to study therapist and client reflections on their mutual interaction. Important here is that the interviews happened soon after the end of the interaction; optimally, this would occur immediately, but not later than within 48 hours, while the memory is still fresh (Elliott, 1986).

Recording-assisted recall is typically embedded in a design in which participant reflection is coupled with an observation-based analysis of the actual original interaction (e.g., a therapy session). Of interest here may be the convergence, divergence, interrelatedness, or disconnection of reported experiences, particularly if recall interviews are conducted independently with the different parties to the interaction being examined (e.g., client and therapist). For instance, a client may be asked to identify helpful events using a recording of a just-finished session (see Elliott & Shapiro, 1988; Timulak & Lietaer, 2001). Once they find an event, they delineate its beginning, end, and peak elements (most helpful responses). The client is then interviewed about why the event was helpful, how they saw the therapist's action in the event, and so forth. The same event is then played for the therapist (without knowing what the client said about the event), who is asked how they saw the client in the event, what they were trying to accomplish in the event, and so forth.

Open-Ended Self-Report Questionnaires

In our experience, written self-report questionnaires are used in qualitative research much less than interviews or focus groups. Data produced using this format are typically distinguished by two related qualities. First, the data are thinner; open-ended self-report questionnaires usually yield less information because participants are not encouraged to elaborate and feel less pressure to express themselves than they would in an interview. However, the data they produce can be quite meaning dense, in that a lot is said in a small number of words. Thus, written self-report questionnaires are often challenging to analyze because the written account does not allow follow-up questions to clarify responses that might be unclear. In our experience, written self-report questionnaires yield more unclear and ambiguous data than interviews conducted by skilled interviewers. This makes them more challenging to analyze, an issue we take up in Chapter 4.

Despite these significant drawbacks, open-ended self-report questionnaires can be invaluable, especially in large or mixed-methods studies, where they are easy to administer to large numbers of people (e.g., Richards & Timulak, 2012) and because they can be powerfully combined with other forms of data collection. For example, it is common in empirical phenomenology (mentioned in Chapter 1) to ask potential participants to first complete a written account of their experience before interviewing them in depth (Wertz, 1983). A useful example of a stand-alone open-ended self-report questionnaire in qualitative psychotherapy research is the Helpful Aspects of Therapy (HAT) Form (Elliott et al., 2006; Llewelyn, 1988; Richards & Timulak, 2012), which asks clients to identify helpful or hindering events in therapy sessions. In addition to generating data for qualitative analysis, the HAT Form can also be combined with recording-assisted recall (e.g., Elliott & Shapiro, 1988) to collect rich data for understanding significant therapy events (see the previous section). The questions used in written self-report questionnaires follow similar rules to those outlined for verbal interviews (e.g., being open ended, unambiguous); however, given the likelihood that participants will not elaborate much, it is even more important to be succinct and limit the number of questions (e.g., less is more). It can also be helpful to embed some instructions that might encourage clarity and prompt elaboration in some detail (e.g., "Please explain your answer").

Observation Notes and Recorded Interactions as Qualitative Data

Although observation as a tool for collecting data has a rich tradition in qualitative research in anthropology and sociology (e.g., ethnography), it is sometimes forgotten in psychology. Indeed, we have had the experience of a reviewer criticizing a paper because the study did not use an interview and thus could not be regarded as qualitative research. This is deeply ironic, given that Glaser and Strauss (1967) developed grounded theory as a method for analyzing observational data. When using observational methods, researchers may take field notes to represent interactions, although it is now more typical to transcribe video or audio recordings. Although observation notes may be quite descriptive, they are naturally interwoven with the observer's interpretations so that it becomes critical to distinguish between description and interpretation (Taylor et al., 2015). Our preference is to dispense with observational notes and work directly with recordings of interactions.

Qualitative observation of either live or recorded interactions has to be guided by an observation protocol that defines domains of investigation, which can be structured theoretically, pragmatically, temporarily, and so forth. As with formulating interview schedules, creating a useful observation protocol requires some conceptual work preceding observation itself, but in turn, conceptualization may be informed and shaped by the observations made. For instance, we may look at client process, therapist process, and client–therapist interactions in client-identified significant events, relying on a general background theory informing observations and interpretation (e.g., Timulak & Lietaer, 2001). Alternatively, we may use a particular theory to structure our observations—for instance, the theory of emotion-focused therapy, which distinguishes among client secondary emotions, primary emotions, unmet needs, and so forth—within the explicitly stated context of a theory that defines those concepts (e.g., O'Brien et al., 2019). Useful guidance on qualitative observation methods can be found in a variety of sources, including Emerson et al. (2011), Guest et al. (2013), Patton (2015), and Taylor et al. (2015); however, for us, the main point is that recorded interactions (especially video recordings) represent an underappreciated but rich source of qualitative information that is worthy of more attention by qualitative researchers.

ANTICIPATING AND ADDRESSING ETHICAL ISSUES

As in all forms of research, in GDI-QR, it is important to carefully consider ethical issues when designing the study and maintain an ethical awareness throughout the process of recruiting participants, collecting and analyzing the data, and even in interpreting and writing up the results. First, you will have to familiarize yourself with key ethical issues that are likely to emerge, which you will have to discuss in your ethics application to your local research ethics committee. What would a typical person have to know about the study to make an informed decision about whether to take part? What are the possible risks and benefits for the participants, and how well do they balance? How will confidentiality or anonymity be created and maintained? What situational pressures (both obvious and subtle) might compromise the ability of prospective participants to say no to taking part, and how can these be minimized? At the same time, we are not aware of any ethical issues specific to the descriptive-interpretive approaches to qualitative research.

Ethical Balance

It is always useful to do a risk assessment in which you lay out the possible risks and benefits for your participants. First, what, if anything, are they likely to gain from taking part? Fortunately, as Kvale (1996) and others have pointed out, when properly done, qualitative research generally provides participants with a safe space in which to reflect on and make meaning out of important experiences; such experiences can even be empowering for participants. In addition, many participants derive pleasure from feeling that they are helping others by taking part. However, there are risks and costs. Most commonly, if the topic is emotionally painful, frightening, private, sensitive, or embarrassing for the participant, some level of emotional distress during or after data collection can be expected. In addition, for various reasons, some clients find completing open-ended qualitative questionnaires like the HAT Form to be burdensome. Finally, some prospective participants might feel pressured to agree to participate, even though they do not want to. Although generally mild, these risks to the ethical principles of beneficence and autonomy are inherent in specific modes of qualitative data collection and recruitment situations; all we can do about them is warn prospective participants, allow them to choose for themselves, and do our best to address them if they occur. The other main risk in GDI-QR is violation of confidentiality, leading to feelings of betrayal and loss of trust. It is important to do everything in our power to secure and anonymize our participants' confidential data. This also includes secure storage (and transfer, if needed) of the data. In Europe, this may involve conforming with the General Data Protection Regulations, the European Union guide for the use of personal data. (For more, see British Psychological Society, 2018).

Informed Consent

If we do our best to be transparent with prospective participants about possible benefits and risks or costs and how we are going to do our best to reduce those risks and help them manage them, then we have done most of the up-front work on the ethical aspects of the research. The other important issue is avoiding implicit pressure for people to agree to take part in our study, to enable them to make a truly free choice to take part or not. That is why it is a good idea to design in a "cooling off" period for people to absorb the information about our study and reflect whether they truly want to participate. It may sound strange, but we feel that it is important to celebrate people saying no to taking part in our research; their refusal means that they have exercised their power, and for us, that is more important than our research. As one of Robert's old professors once said to him, "Never forget that people are more important than your research!" (For more on ethical issues in qualitative research, see Iphofen & Tolich, 2018.)

BUILDING IN INTEGRITY CHECKS

Given our critical realist epistemological position and our background in the discipline of psychotherapy research (see Chapter 1), which has a strong quantitative mainstream, we are strong advocates for improving the quality of qualitative research through the use of various procedures that are best planned in advance. We thus advocate that the planning phase of a GDI-QR study includes figuring out what kinds of methodological integrity checks (see Chapter 6) are to be included to enhance the richness of our data, the accuracy of our transcriptions, and the credibility of our findings. For example, how much time has to be devoted to training and checking on interviewers and data analysts? Will you use multiple qualitative analysts working in parallel to one another, or will auditing by the main supervisor be sufficient? The researchers may, for instance, use a feedback loop on how the interviewer behaves in the interview, the study may also use more interviewers, the interviewers and transcribers of interviews may be different people, and so forth. In the case of studies using observations, how many observers are likely to be needed? Will there be a feedback loop in which observers get feedback on their observations from a coresearcher who was not involved in the initial observations? These and other integrity checks specific to the main study analysis process are described in more detail in Chapter 4.

We also advocate various forms of triangulation in which multiple perspectives or kinds of information are brought to bear on the data. For instance, we can situate (describe) the sample through quantitative means (e.g., to select empowerment events on the basis of them being rated as empowering by the clients using a standard quantitative scale; see Timulak & Elliott, 2003). We can also use several perspectives on the data using various researchers or analysts and auditors, primarily to correct errors of transcription or get feedback on our interpretation. To make our data richer and more nuanced and to bring out ambiguities and contradictions, we can combine data from self-report and observation (many of our significant event studies combined perspectives of clients, therapists, and observers; e.g., Elliott, 1984; Elliott & Shapiro, 1992; Elliott et al., 1994; Labott et al., 1992; Timulak & Lietaer, 2001; Timulak & Elliott, 2003). Using other methods of triangulation, such as seeking feedback from the original participants or comparing qualitative descriptions with outcome, is also possible. During the planning phase, it is also useful to challenge your planned research design by applying a methodological integrity framework to it (e.g., Elliott et al., 1999; Levitt, Motulsky, et al., 2017; see also Chapter 6, this volume). The point we are making here is that the time to build in integrity checks is before you start collecting data rather than after the fact, when your options are likely to be much more limited.

SUMMARY OF KEY POINTS

In this chapter, we have tried to make a case for careful planning in the descriptive-interpretive approach. We strongly advocated for devoting time and energy to defining the research topic and questions that will guide your investigation, getting familiar with the relevant research literature, and carefully spelling out your expectations and likely biases (or preunderstandings). We also discussed the benefits of putting together a team of researchers. We then supported the use of a wide range of data collection formats, including different types of interviews (individual, focus group, recording-assisted), open-ended self-report questionnaires, and observation (using transcripts of recorded interactions). We concluded by highlighting ethical issues and methodological integrity issues essential to designing a descriptive-interpretive qualitative study.

3 COLLECTING THE DATA

In this chapter, we present how our generic approach to descriptive-interpretive qualitative research (GDI-QR) looks at the data collection process, beginning with how organizing theoretical frameworks (including research domains) are developed, then taking up the piloting of the data collection protocol, before moving on to the researcher-informant relationship and concluding with the idea that data collection itself, especially skilled qualitative interviewing and observation, is a form of analysis. In the process, we deliberately blur the boundaries between data collection and analysis, anticipating some of the modes of qualitative data analysis we discuss in Chapter 4.

DEVELOPING THE ORGANIZING CONCEPTUAL FRAMEWORK FOR THE RESEARCH ("DOMAINS")

In general, the scholarly work that led to the formulation of the research problem and relevant research questions (see Chapter 2) also guides the researchers in structuring how they collect data. This structuring may

https://doi.org/10.1037/0000224-003
Essentials of Descriptive-Interpretive Qualitative Research: A Generic Approach,
by R. Elliott and L. Timulak
Copyright © 2021 by the American Psychological Association. All rights reserved.

be theoretically led, as long as the researcher makes sure that the theory that informs data collection (e.g., distinguishing between essentialist [i.e., in-born] and cultural vs. constructed aspects of gender identity as understood in feminist-critical theory) is permeable enough that it can be altered by emerging data.

It is important for researchers to be clear about and aware of what is informing their data collection strategy, including during the actual gathering of data in the moment (e.g., during an interview, attempts to clarify what a participant is saying; see the section Data Collection as Continuous Analysis later in this chapter). For instance, an emotion-focused researcher is going to be influenced by the emotion scheme model (Elliott et al., 2004) and so asks a participant about a feeling in terms of questions such as, "What were you feeling?" "What did you react to?" "What did you feel in your body?" "What was it telling you about what you needed in the situation?" Similarly, a feminist-critical researcher might ask questions about development, gender identity, social context, discrimination, and resilience (Levitt, Surace, et al., 2018).

The questions used in the data collection protocol (interview, questionnaire, or observation guide) point toward broad topics of investigation. Following Glaser (1978; he called them "formal categories"), we define *domain structure* as the set of broad topics of investigation that define what the researcher is interested in learning about. In a sense, they tell the researcher where to look but not what to find there. They can be framed as researcher questions and subquestions; the point of the research is to find answers to these research questions. Domains are typically formulated on the basis of an initial conceptualization at the beginning of data collection. This conceptualization may be *pragmatically* led (e.g., within the study of schizophrenia we may be interested in finding out "what helps or hinders the process of recovery"; e.g., Davidson, 2003), *temporarily* formulated (e.g., "What happened before your first episode, during it, and afterward?"), or *theoretically* informed (e.g., in the context of a mindfulness study, asking participants about their self-treatment: "How would you say you treated yourself before the group started?"; L'Estrange et al., 2016), and so forth. Whichever of these might be the case, it is important that researchers are clear with themselves and their later audience regarding how their domains of investigation were determined and how these formulations and domains of investigation affected the data collection process.

Why are we so strongly in favor of making conceptual frameworks more central to qualitative research? On the face of it, such advice appears to go against the whole point of qualitative research, which is to explore human experiences and actions in an open-ended, discovery-oriented way. Our advice might sound to some as a selling out of the promise of qualitative research, even a betrayal. We could be seen as smuggling the hypothetical-deductive method and the rest of the positivist enterprise back into qualitative research. Our main purpose is to help you avoid one of the most common and serious pitfalls we have observed in qualitative research: mistaking the researchers' implicit conceptual structure for the findings or results of the study (see Timulak & Elliott, 2019). All too often, we find ourselves frustrated by qualitative studies that report findings that are essentially the domains of investigation or even the main focus the researchers wanted to explore in the first place. For instance, the researchers may claim that they wanted to study therapists' experiences of "a good therapy hour"; then, after all their time-consuming analyses, they report that the main "theme," or core category in their study, was "a good therapy hour."

To recap, we recommend that researchers organize their data into domains of investigation. A useful illustration of the latter comes from one of Laco's studies (Timulak et al., 2017), in which he and his colleagues explored clients' experiences of emotion-focused therapy (EFT) for generalized anxiety and the changes due to that therapy (see Exhibit 3.1). The nature of the phenomenon under investigation and the context of the discipline (psychotherapy) pointed to a set of key questions that might be useful for informing and strengthening a new treatment (in this example, EFT for generalized anxiety). In particular, it was of clear interest to gather information from clients about the impact of their therapy and what they felt worked or did not work in this therapy. The qualitative part of this study thus delineated four domains of investigation: changes due to therapy, helpful aspects of therapy, unhelpful aspects of therapy, and difficult but helpful aspects of therapy. These domains of investigation mapped onto the research questions and the actual interview questions (derived from the

EXHIBIT 3.1. Example of Pragmatically Based Domains of Investigation

Domain of Investigation (Conceptual Framework)

Changes due to therapy
Helpful aspects of therapy
Unhelpful aspects of therapy
Difficult but helpful aspects of therapy

Note. Adapted from "Emotion-Focused Therapy for Generalized Anxiety Disorder: An Exploratory Study," by L. Timulak, J. McElvaney, D. Keogh, E. Martin, P. Clare, E. Chepukova, and L. S. Greenberg, 2017, *Psychotherapy*, 54(4), p. 363 (https://doi.org/10.1037/pst0000128). Copyright 2017 by the American Psychological Association.

Client Change Interview; Elliott, 2008): For example, "What changes, if any, have you noticed in yourself since therapy started? Can you sum up what has been helpful about your therapy? What kinds of things about the therapy have been hindering, unhelpful, negative, or disappointing for you? Were there things in the therapy that were difficult or painful but still okay or perhaps helpful? What were they?" The clients' answers were then assigned to one or more of the four domains. (Domains do not have to be mutually exclusive, but as it happened, in this study, they were.)

The conceptual framework may also derive from the logical structure of a phenomenon (including who is involved and its temporal structure), as illustrated by Timulak and Elliott (2003; see Exhibit 3.2), who looked at empowerment events (in-session therapy episodes that led to client experiences of empowerment) in EFT for depression. After identifying therapy events that were both nominated as helpful and also rated as empowering by clients on a post-session questionnaire, clients and therapists reviewed those events using brief structured recall (BSR; Elliott & Shapiro, 1988), which consisted of open-ended recall interview questions and some quantitative instruments. Those events were then analyzed using the data from BSR as well as session transcripts. All the available pertinent data were divided between the following domains: (a) client problematic process (preceding session), (b) client in-session process, (c) therapist in-session process and therapeutic interaction, and (d) the event impact on the client (including feeling empowered). The delineation of the domains here had to do with the nature of individual psychotherapy, where we have two participants in different roles (a person in need—the client—and a helper—the therapist), as well as a standard representation of the temporal process of therapy in which a client problematic process provides the prior context for a set of

EXHIBIT 3.2. Example of Domains of Investigation Based on the Logical Structure of the Phenomenon Being Studied

Domain of Investigation (Conceptual Framework)

1. Client problematic process (prior to session; e.g., sad experience concerning a relationship)
2. Client in-session process (e.g., gives voice to part of self)
3. Therapist in-session process and therapeutic interaction (e.g., empathically and evocatively follows client experience)
4. Event impact on client (e.g., feeling of hopefulness and determination)

Note. From "Empowerment Events in Process-Experiential Psychotherapy of Depression: An Exploratory Qualitative Analysis," by L. Timulak and R. Elliott, 2003, *Psychotherapy Research*, 13(4), pp. 449–450 (https://doi.org/10.1093/ptr/kpg043). Copyright 2003 by Taylor & Francis. Adapted with permission.

in-session client and therapist processes, which gives rise to a set of impacts or reactions on the part of the client. Each event was then analyzed through the outlined domains.

PILOTING THE DATA COLLECTION PROTOCOL

The main feature of GDI-QR (and practically all qualitative research approaches) is that it uses an open-ended data-gathering strategy, whereby we seek to unfold detailed descriptive information about a phenomenon. This means that even though the researcher will have some preunderstandings and even an organizing conceptual framework for the phenomenon, it is important that they try to facilitate the emergence of different and detailed understandings. Often, this also involves allowing oneself as a researcher to be guided by participants, particularly in the various interview formats.

To this end, it is useful for the researcher to pilot a new interview or observation schedule before beginning serious data collection, so they can get some sense about how participants are likely to understand and respond to the questions. The researcher may want to know from participants whether the study inquiry is overlooking something of importance or whether they have any suggestions as to what the study should focus its inquiry on. This can be done in the form of additional questions in the research interview, when the participant may be asked questions such as "Is there something we did not ask you that we should have?" "What is your perspective on the questions we asked you?" It is important for the researcher to be alert to information that participants feel they have to tell the researcher for the researcher to understand them better. For example, Robert added a "Difficult but OK" question to the Client Change Interview (Elliott et al., 2001) because when he asked clients whether there was anything in their therapy that they found hindering or unhelpful, they repeatedly responded by saying, "Well, it wasn't hindering, but it certainly was difficult when my therapist . . ." All too often, researchers do not attend carefully to the nuances and sources of their research interview questions. Poorly or ambiguously worded interview or questionnaire items lead to uninformative or confusing data.

SAMPLING, SELECTING, AND RECRUITING PARTICIPANTS

The logic of sample selection in qualitative research is usually described as differing from that of quantitative research. In quantitative research, inference from the sample to the population is carried out using statistical methods and analyzing the representativeness of the sample in reference to the target population it represents. The fact that such methods are rarely used (Barker et al., 2015) and deeply flawed (Siegfried, 2010) is the topic for another book. In contrast, in qualitative research, claims about generalizability or transferability (Stiles, 2003) of findings to the population tend to be considerably more modest. That does not mean that we are giving up on generalizing our findings beyond the sample, as is at times falsely implied in some qualitative studies we have come across. After all, the word "sample" implies that there is a larger population from which participants were selected and that we are interested in saying something about. It simply means that we want to be careful about any such inferences.

Therefore, in GDI-QR, the first thing is for researchers to systematically record the characteristics of their participants as they go, writing down any contextual or otherwise relevant details (including information about recruitment) that may later play a role in shaping findings. These may include gender identification, age, ethnicity, education, work, clinical presentation, and so on. (We say more about this in Chapter 5, where we discuss writing up the study.)

As we have outlined elsewhere (Timulak & Elliott, 2019), at a minimum, we want to be able to talk about what is possible (what form a phenomenon can have). Asserting that a particular phenomenon exists is a relatively modest knowledge claim and is therefore not hard to sustain. If you are doing a qualitative case study to document the existence of a particular phenomenon (such as an intense moment of weeping in therapy; e.g., Labott et al., 1992), you do not have to worry too much about representativeness; you just need a few relevant details. How likely or common something is (how representative features of the phenomenon are) is more difficult to determine, and in general, qualitative researchers do not aspire to answer such questions. Even when we offer an account of how representative some finding was within our sample (see Chapter 4), we do so primarily to inform the reader and provide contextual detail that might help the reader evaluate our abductive leap from data to potentially generalizable concept (Rennie, 2012).

In terms of sample size, we see the concept of *saturation* as broadly applicable and useful in our generic approach. According to grounded theory analysis, analysis of a phenomenon can be said to be saturated when new categories stop emerging and the relationships among the categories have been identified (Glaser & Strauss, 1967). Where possible, we can try to analyze available data and outline provisional findings and thus see whether added data bring further alterations in our provisional conceptualization.

This can be particularly handy in the case of interview-generated data. We can conduct an interview with 10 to 12 participants, analyze the data, outline the emerging conceptualization (e.g., descriptions, themes, categories), then add another two to three participants and see whether the newly generated data bring any new descriptions, themes, or categories. This process can be repeated until our findings become stable and new data do not alter them (see Chapter 4).

This is the ideal; obviously, in reality, there are pragmatic issues that have to be addressed and data collection deadlines to be met, and so these may play a large role in determining our sample and its size. For instance, many qualitative studies in psychotherapy research are nested within other designs, such as randomized controlled trials (e.g., Richards & Timulak, 2012). At other times, qualitative studies may focus on a single event or episode, such as the Dutch painter van Gogh's cutting off his ear (Runyan, 1982), considering all contextual information, such as the person's relevant life history and current situation and details of the episode itself and its sequelae so that the sheer amount of information requires a focus on one or a small number of events. (For a therapy research example, see Rees et al., 2001.)

Nevertheless, an attempt at saturation may tell us how stable and generalizable our findings (e.g., emerging conceptualization, descriptions, themes, categories) are likely to be, at least within the realm of participants such as those included in our sample. In any case, the researcher should offer a thorough reflection on what influenced their sampling, what characterizes their sample, what implications these factors have for their findings, and what the reader might wish to consider when transferring or generalizing the findings to other contexts.

For instance, in our study of empowering events in EFT (Timulak & Elliott, 2003), we analyzed processes in a collection of 12 significant events involving nine clients; these events were selected from a larger pool of helpful significant events ($N = 103$) nominated by the clients from a larger study on EFT for depression ($N = 48$), using the Helpful Aspects of Therapy Form (Llewelyn, 1988). The clients and therapists underwent a mixed-methods interpersonal process recall interview (BSR; Elliott & Shapiro, 1988) asking them about their experiences and understandings of the processes present in the event. A section of the BSR involved assessing their feelings during the event on a quantitative Client Feelings Scale, which contained the item "powerful/hopeful/active." We selected the 12 events in which the clients gave the maximum rating on the 5-point scale from *not at all* to *pretty much*. These 12 events then constituted the sample on which we conducted a detailed and thorough qualitative analysis using all the data from BSR.

In the published article (Timulak & Elliott, 2003), we provided further available quantitative data (e.g., the overall outcome on outcome measures and mean ratings on the Client Feelings Scale) to help situate our sample of 12 events and nine clients in the context of the larger pool of helpful events ($N = 103$) and depressed clients ($N = 48$). Thus, we were able to situate our sample for later readers to help them make an interpretive leap from our findings to a range of similar events and clients.

THE RESEARCH ALLIANCE

Almost all forms of qualitative data collection discussed here occur in some kind of relational context, which can strongly affect the nature and quality of the data collected from participants. This working research alliance between researcher and participant is fostered by several factors, many of which are also ethical principles, including, most important, researcher-offered relational qualities such as empathy, respect, authenticity, curiosity, and competence. Researchers can also build this research alliance by treating participants fairly and ethically; devoting time to the consent process; offering a safe, boundaried space for data collection; keeping time-boundaries; ensuring confidentiality; providing emotional support or encouragement when needed; and so on. These considerations apply not only to the various interview-based formats (qualitative interviews, focus groups, tape-assisted recall) but also to observation and even open-ended self-report questionnaires (questionnaires create virtual relationships).

More specifically, a good qualitative interview in part resembles person-centered counseling and thus contains a strong relational element and is governed by similar ethical principles (e.g., American Psychological Association, 2017). However, the goal here is not necessarily for the participant to feel understood and emotionally supported, but rather to feel validated and encouraged to elaborate and provide further detail. Verbal responses that communicate empathic understanding (e.g., "So, you felt so understood by your sponsor") by the interviewer are coupled with further inquiry and probing for further detail (e.g., "So, could you tell me what conveyed that sense of being understood?"). The interviewer wants to unfold the participant's account and so facilitates the participant to elaborate and explain. The interview is thus also often supplemented by encouragements (e.g., "Could you tell me more?" "Could you give me an example?" "Could you explain further?" "Was there anything else that was helpful?"). The interviewer seeks to be both engaged and inquisitive, demonstrating interest in the participant's experience and an openness to hearing whatever that experience might be. The interviewer also has to be aware of any potential dynamic between themselves and the participant. This may include cultural or contextual considerations depending on the subject of the interview and the persons involved. For instance, the interviewer may reflect on how they can be perceived doing an interview in a homeless shelter. They may check in advance with staff about what they should be aware of for their presentation before the interview. The interviewer may also have to be ready to provide emotional support to the participant, particularly if the topic is sensitive. So, an appropriate debriefing should be a natural part of any research interview.

DATA COLLECTION AS CONTINUOUS ANALYSIS

Good qualitative interviewing is not an automatic, mechanical process but instead involves a literal or metaphoric dialogue with sources of our data. It inevitably involves a degree of analytical work on the part of the interviewer, in which the researcher listens mindfully to the informant, reflects back and checks their understandings with the person, questions unclarities, and, in particular, listens to determine what question the informant is actually answering, which may be quite different from the question asked by the researcher. Even in the case of extracting archival data, the researcher makes sure to supply missing contextual information. We say more about "pre-analysis" activities in Chapter 4; for now, we simply want to note that data collection and data analysis overlap and cannot be completely separated from one another.

The following is an example of continuous analysis by the researcher during a Client Change Interview with a socially anxious client from one of Robert's studies.

INTERVIEWER: What about things in therapy that have been hindering or unhelpful or negative or disappointing?

CLIENT: Um, well, I probably . . . in the time I've—now and again— I've felt I've been with him [*the therapist*], I've just felt that I annoyed him, I irritated him . . . [but] when I say it's hindered me, maybe really it hasn't hindered me because it's made me think about it when I've gone away and realized.

INTERVIEWER: Right, so in the moment, it's sort of got in the way.

CLIENT: Uh-huh.

INTERVIEWER: But then actually on reflection about it, it allows you to really see that dynamic being played out . . .

CLIENT: Uh-huh, yeah, so it's, so that's the thing, it's not . . .

INTERVIEWER: Sort of a combination of helpful, but also hindering at the same time.

SUMMARY OF KEY POINTS

In this chapter on data collection, we have highlighted the importance of three preliminary steps: developing an articulated conceptual framework of domains, pilot testing the data collection protocol, and developing a clear strategy for sampling and recruiting participants. We then identified two key aspects of the data collection process: development of a safe, boundaried, ethical working alliance between participant and researcher and mindful attention to the informativeness and clarity of participants' answers to the researcher's questions (which in turn express the guiding domains or interests of the researcher).

4

A FRAMEWORK OF KEY MODES OF QUALITATIVE DATA ANALYSIS

In this chapter, we go considerably beyond what we have previously written about our generic account of descriptive-interpretive qualitative data analysis (Elliott & Timulak, 2005). We present a detailed, systematic account of the range of analysis modes, drawing together what we see as the most common and useful practices from grounded theory analysis (Strauss & Corbin, 1998), empirical phenomenology (Wertz, 1983), and consensual qualitative research (Hill et al., 1997), among others. At the end of this chapter, we offer a pithier, less systematic list of aphorisms that try to capture some of our hard-won learnings on what qualitative data analysis is really about (if you want to peek ahead, see Exhibit 4.3).

Because it is a generic approach applicable to diverse phenomena, scientific disciplines, and methodological contexts, we assume there will also be a lot of variability in the ways researchers, following our recommendations, would analyze their data. Therefore, the outline we provide here is only suggestive, and we assume individual researchers will rely on particular considerations to shape their ways of analyzing data. Flexibility and creativity are central to the approach, the main goal of which is to address

https://doi.org/10.1037/0000224-004
Essentials of Descriptive-Interpretive Qualitative Research: A Generic Approach,
by R. Elliott and L. Timulak
Copyright © 2021 by the American Psychological Association. All rights reserved.

the research problem at hand as carefully and informatively as possible. This means that we invite researchers to apply critical reflection throughout the research process (see Elliott & Timulak, 2005). By *critical reflection*, we mean a reflective process that is cautious and questions our assumptions, the analytic methods used, and the emerging findings.

The four overarching data analysis modes or activities are, broadly speaking, pre-analysis, understanding and translating, categorizing, and integrating. Each of these overarching modes groups together sets of related activities, as outlined in Exhibit 4.1 and explained in detail in the numbered sections of this chapter. Although these modes have a rough sequential order, in practice, they overlap. As we have been emphasizing, the process is flexible, and individual studies may deal with circumstances that have an impact on the sequence of these steps. The procedure is, however, systematic, reflected on, and recorded throughout. The approach also includes relevant integrity checks throughout the process (see also Chapters 2 and 6).

PRE-ANALYSIS ACTIVITIES

1. Organizing Data Into Domains of Investigation

Once the researchers define their data set, we recommend that they start to organize data into a conceptual framework based on the domains of investigation, as described in much more detail in Chapter 3. (In some cases, this may be preceded by delineating meaning units, which we describe in the section titled Data Preparation.) As noted, this conceptual framework is initially informed by the researchers' preunderstandings about the phenomenon, as well as their research questions and a combination of the logical structure of the phenomenon and existing broad theory (e.g., emotion-focused therapy [EFT] emotion theory). However, domain structures can and should be modified along the way as new broad aspects of the phenomenon emerge.

2. Data Collection (as Continuous Analysis)

As we pointed out in Chapter 3, collection of data in qualitative research is not mechanical but instead involves a process of continuous analysis. We thus list data collection as a mode of analysis to underscore this important truth about qualitative research: In the case of qualitative interviewing, it requires active, engaged listening and empathic feedback to the informant and, in particular, listening carefully to hear what question the informant is answering (rather than the question they were asked). By the same token,

EXHIBIT 4.1. A Generic Approach to Qualitative Data Analysis: Analysis Modes

A. Pre-analysis (all studies need these)

   1. Organizing data into domains of investigation: critical and continuing reflection on our organizing research questions and implicit or explicit theory about the phenomenon, leading to formulation of guiding investigatory domains (see Chapter 3)

   2. Data collection: continuous analysis; reflect back to informant, check understandings, question unclarities, provide missing contextual information (see Chapter 3)

   3. Data preparation: (a) transcription, (b) judgment of relevance, (c) delineation of meaning units

B. Understanding and translating (researchers select one or more primary analysis modes)

   4. Meaning unit summary: meaning condensation—describing the gist, boiling the meaning down; translating into briefer language

   5. Explicating implicit meaning: bringing out what is said "between the lines," what is understood by the speakers in their context; not nonconscious meaning

   6. Interpreting nonconscious meaning: using an explicit interpretive theory (e.g., psychoanalysis, feminist-Marxist theory, emotion theory) to intentionally read beyond informant's awareness

   7. Process description: characterizing the nature of the informant's observable speech action or manner (e.g., minimizing, playing up; narrative actions)

C. Categorizing: Creating and working with categories (all studies need these)

   8. Category construction: using similarities to cluster meaning units and categories into themes, categories, and distinctions that accurately describe data; naming the categories; organizing categories into hierarchical trees or structures

   9. Putting meaning units into categories: classifying meaning units into emergent categories (vs. traditional content analysis, which classifies data into a priori categories)

   10. Running integrity checks on the analysis: systematically evaluating categories by checking for fit with the data and coherent structure (auditing), within-sample spread (enumerating categories), divergence from researcher expectations, and if appropriate, agreement by other researchers (consensus)

D. Integrating the findings (all studies need this)

   11. Depicting structure and providing summary narratives: pulling the analysis together to show how the categories relate to one another; using graphic representations (diagrams, flow charts), or telling an interesting, compelling story from the analysis

qualitative observation (e.g., while watching video recordings of interactions) is also an active process in which the researcher scans the interaction being observed for relevant information, trying to read not only what is being said but also what is implied.

3. Data Preparation

After data collection, the researchers transcribe their data, determine what data are relevant to the study, and divide their data into meaning units.

3a. Transcription

Every data analysis requires prior preparation of data. Qualitative data do not just fall out of the sky, a gift of the gods to be accepted uncritically and with gratitude. They are more like Trojan horses or, more accurately, wild horses: We have to understand where they came from and also to corral, win over, and tame them—but not too much, lest their spirit is lost. Some of this is obvious: The data have to be transferred from more fragile, less accessible media (audio or video recordings or scribbled postsession questionnaires) to more permanent, accessible media (written digitized transcripts). And yet, even something so apparently transparent as transcription involves important, theory-driven decisions, such as the level and kind of detail about verbal and nonverbal behavior to include (e.g., whether to count pauses or distinguish in-breaths from sighs).

In most cases, transcription for qualitative research is focused on the content of what informants say, as opposed to the process of how they say it. The researcher works with the informant's words as an account of their experience, so a *content transcript* is what they need. The microdetails of researcher–informant interaction are not of interest; transcribing these will simply get in the researcher's way, distracting them with irrelevancies. In a content transcript, it is a good idea to edit out speech nonfluencies and exact repetitions. To illustrate what we mean, we provide the following example of a microanalytic transcript of part of a significant weeping event (Labott et al., 1992), ideal for studying the moment-by-moment intricacies of client–therapist interaction (for transcription symbols, see Sacks et al., 1974):

> C88 (Peak): I don't think that I ever accepted that, I think what I did was I ass- I think (1.1 sec) I think I assumed, that I went from (1.4 sec) if he's violent and (shaky voice:) angry, then that's where the love °got taken away°, in the violence and the anger, of his drinking (crying) IT WAS GONE! (Labott et al., 1992, p. 52)

In contrast, the following is a cleaned-up content transcript of the same segment, which is more streamlined and easier to read but lacks richness and drama:

C88.1 (Peak): I don't think that I ever accepted that [abuse by my father]. I think what I did was I assumed that I went from, if he's violent and angry, then that's where the love got taken away. In the violence and the anger of his drinking it was gone.

If your focus is on the content of the person's experience, the second version is much easier to work with, especially with the addition of bracketed explications of implied meanings.

3b. Judgment of Relevance

In our approach to preparing data for qualitative analysis, we follow empirical phenomenology (Wertz, 1983) by being explicit that part of the researcher's job is to go through the collected data and retain only what is relevant in some way for the study. The scope of the study is defined by its research problem and research questions. When the data are gathered, a lot of information may get collected that has no relevance for the study. For instance, we may conduct a research interview on the clients' experiences of therapy, and as we start our recording, the clients may start to talk about the weather or their journey to the venue where the interview is being conducted, and so on. There may also be situational comments that happen during the interview that are not relevant for the study itself as well (e.g., somebody enters the interview room). The same may apply to the data collected through observation. Therefore, we recommend that the researchers get familiar with their data, inspect the transcribed data in their entirety, and retain only the data relevant for their study, which will then become the study data. When doing this, the researchers have to ensure that they have recorded the guidelines they used for deciding whether something was considered relevant data.

Furthermore, the overall process is systematic and organized so that all the relevant data that are used in the analysis are traceable to their source. This part is important because we are advocates of using all available study data. At times, we come across studies conducted by other researchers where it is not clear whether all relevant available study data were used in the analysis or whether the findings are based on selectively used data (see qualitative analysis secret 1, Exhibit 4.3 at the end of this chapter). Therefore, we suggest that once the researchers define what constitutes their relevant data, they establish some kind of tracking system that shows the sources of each category or finding. (We say more about this shortly.)

3c. Delineation of Meaning Units

Meaning units (Giorgi, 1985; Rennie et al., 1988; Wertz, 1983) are the smallest units used in generic descriptive-interpretive qualitative research (GDI-QR). Although some qualitative approaches divide the data into smaller units (e.g., clauses) or arbitrary units (e.g., individual lines of transcribed text), we recommend that the smallest units of data be complete thoughts capable of standing alone and sufficiently developed that they are capable of communicating a message (meaning) relevant to one or more of the study's research questions. Meaning units often approximate sentences; however, sentences can be too short to communicate the intended meaning fully. Similarly, some forms of qualitative research (e.g., interpretative phenomenological analysis; Smith et al., 2009) use line numbers; however, we find these to be arbitrary and worry that they may change when document font or format is altered. Therefore, we recommend breaking the data into units ranging from complete sentences to small paragraphs capable of communicating a clear message. One recommended strategy is to introduce a break in the text when a new meaning is expressed.

The process of deciding where one meaning ends and the new one starts is inevitably a subjective or analytic decision made by the researcher, and the same researcher may change their mind depending on their frame of mind and the stage of analysis. We have also found that qualitative analysts vary widely in the size of meaning unit that they prefer to work with. Some, like Robert, prefer small, discrete meaning units on the order of sentences and even sometimes clauses, especially at the beginning of an analysis, because they feel precise and manageable; this is consistent with Robert's predilection for close reading of texts and his somewhat obsessive cognitive style. This drives others, such as Laco, crazy and can leave them feeling as if they have lost the forest for the trees. Laco, therefore, prefers larger meaning units, on the order of small paragraphs, because he likes to look at things more globally. This, in turn, bothers Robert because he feels like important details are being skipped over, and you never know when a detail is going to turn out to be important. However, even Robert ends up using bigger meaning units at the end of an analysis project. For instance, a client in a posttherapy interview asking about the changes resulting from therapy may say,

42. Yeah. I am going back to how confident I used to be, for one, and not letting anything really bother me at all. Just, basically, I've just gone back to the way I used to be: this outgoing, confident person.

This can be one meaning unit (Laco's preference) or two (Robert's preference), as follows:

42.1. Yeah. I am going back to how confident I used to be, for one, and not letting anything really bother me at all.

42.2. Just, basically, I've just gone back to the way I used to be: this outgoing, confident person.

In fact, it is always possible at a later stage of the analysis to recombine consecutive meaning units (e.g., 11, 12, and 13 become 11/12/13) or, conversely, to further divide them (e.g., 29 becomes 29a and 29b). The important thing is not to stress yourself about the meaning units stage and especially not to use it to avoid the hard work of the later stages of the analysis.

Meaning Units Can Have Multiple Meanings
It may also happen that the researchers decide that a meaning unit contains more than one meaning. This is especially likely in the case of large meaning units, such as longer paragraphs. However, this need not be a problem, and we advise that, during the process of further analyzing (e.g., clustering) meaning units, consideration be given to the possibility that the same meaning unit may be put into two or more categories (see the section titled Categorizing: Creating and Working With Categories). In other words, analysis need not necessarily lead to mutually exclusive categories (themes). However, larger meaning units with multiple meanings do present certain problems for the analysis process. For one thing, they can be unwieldy, especially for citing as examples in text. For another, readers may not know which part of a larger meaning unit got it into a given category, and even the analyst may struggle to remember this. For this reason, additional strategies are often used with larger meaning units; these may involve the analyst writing a summary label or highlighting the relevant part of the meaning unit (see Meaning Unit Summary in the next section of this chapter). Another problem with large meaning units is that they can lead to overcategorization, in which the same meaning unit gets used repeatedly, leading to blurred or muddy categories.

The delineation of meaning units, in our experience, can be done in the data preparation stage along with the delineation of domains. However, in reality, these steps are often intertwined because the researchers can also discard redundancies in the data when delineating meaning units or tweak domains as a consequence of further engagement with the data while delineating meaning units. Thus, the whole process is fluid. In the same way that a meaning unit may end up in more than one category, it can sometimes also be assigned to more than one domain.

Meaning Unit ID Tags

As noted, we want a clear accounting system showing where each piece of data came from, enabling our categories to be clearly traceable. This should encompass every piece of data (i.e., all of a particular participant's account or a particular observation episode or recording segment). To do this, we recommend that a tracking code is used to identify each meaning unit. This should usually contain an indication of which participant the meaning unit comes from (e.g., Participant A) and a corresponding number (e.g., 1) so it could be distinguished from other meaning units from the same participant. Thus, we would have Participant A with meaning units A1, A2, A3, A4, and so forth, and Participant B with meaning units B1, B2, B3, and so forth. At times, we may need another indicator that meaningfully structures meaning units—in the context of a significant events study, we may have several independent therapy events or sessions included in our data set. We then can have a Participant A, an Event (or Session) 1 that involves that participant, and the Meaning Unit 1 from that participant. The coding would then be A1.1, with further meaning units from the same event being A1.2, A1.3, A1.4, and so forth. Once we have the second event from the same participant, the coding used can be A2.1, A2.2, A2.3, and so forth.

UNDERSTANDING AND TRANSLATING MODES OF ANALYSIS

In our view, there are two central modes of qualitative analysis. One of these is understanding and expressing in words what single meaning units are saying about the phenomenon being studied; the other is creating groupings of meaning units (categories) according to similarities contained in them. These form the heart not just of qualitative analysis but of qualitative research in general. Thus, the essence of qualitative research is understanding and translating and categorizing. As we see it, variations in the first of these main modes, understanding and translating, is what distinguishes the different descriptive-interpretive qualitative approaches from one another; that is, they emphasize different kinds of understanding and translating. Selecting how you are going to understand and translate your data is one of the most important decisions that qualitative researchers have to make in designing studies. In this section, we walk you through the different options and try to give you enough information to make an informed decision about how to proceed.

We think there are four main modes or ways in which qualitative researchers read their data to understand them and translate them into terms that readily lend themselves to categorizing: meaning unit summary, explicating implicit meaning, interpreting nonconscious meaning, and process description. Some of these focus more on getting at the participant's meaning; others try to go beyond that meaning, aided by more general theories about what is important or interesting. All, however, by necessity, rely on and are shaped by the researcher's preunderstandings and domains for investigation.

4. Meaning Unit Summary

The first of these modes of understanding and translating is *meaning unit summary*, referred to as *meaning condensation* in empirical phenomenology (Giorgi, 1985). Here, the researcher reads a meaning unit like a person-centered therapist, aiming to get at the gist or main point of what is being said, then attempts to re-present that meaning in a succinct, concise manner, in effect, boiling the meaning down. For example, Rennie et al. (1988, p. 142) in their version of grounded theory analysis, advocated writing a two- or three-word headline summary of the meaning unit, sometimes referred to as a "code," as the following example shows:

INTERVIEWER: Can you recall what was going on between you and your therapist during this part of the interview?

CLIENT: Well, he was just listening intently. He wasn't commenting very much. I never really let him. Sometimes I interrupt him all the time because I have more to add, you know.

This meaning unit has multiple meanings, which were subsequently condensed down to the following: "Therapist listened intently; client interrupted; more to add." Clearly, meaning unit summary is going to be most useful with larger, paragraph-length meaning units or with data from long-winded or repetitive informants, translating them into briefer, more manageable language, thus overcoming a potential downside of larger meaning units. This form of understanding and translating is possibly the most common and could be considered the normative or default mode for most kinds of qualitative analysis.

5. Explicating Implicit Meaning

Beyond meaning unit summary, there are at least three other ways of under-standing and expressing informant meaning. Robert encountered the first of these in his research on significant therapy events. Here, the problem was not that there were too many words, requiring a process of summarization, but instead, there were too few words, with a lot being left unsaid "between the lines." For example, in the Labott et al. (1992) study of a significant weeping event, cited earlier, the client began by stating the following:

C88.1: I don't think that I ever accepted that. (p. 52)

To fully understand what the client meant here, the researchers had to engage in a process of explicating the implicit meanings that would have been understood by client and therapist in context, referred to as "occasion-level meaning" by Stiles (1986), producing the following translation:

C88.1: In contrast to what I just said, it is now my view that I never (as a child or now as an adult) accepted that someone (such as my father) who truly loved me could also hurt me.

It is generally not difficult to do this; all you have to do is listen to enough of the context preceding the meaning unit to know what the speakers are talking about; in effect, you are simply supplying the missing contextual information that was lost when you took the meaning unit out of its context. Once the implicit meaning is brought out, it is easier to see what is going on. For example, we hear that the client in the preceding example senses a contradiction or internal conflict and that she is discussing an unresolved traumatic event or emotional trigger involving a significant other.

Explicating the ideas of the important pieces of qualitative data is a hermeneutic (i.e., interpretive) process of completing the speaker's act of reference. When people speak, they seldom state explicitly all they mean, leaving much to be read "between the lines." These include taken-for-granted knowledge or beliefs that are assumed to be shared by the other person, references to previously described or shared events, omitted logical steps in chains of reasoning presumed to be "too obvious" (or sometimes too shaky!) to be worth mentioning, and what is suggested to others via stylistic cues such as sarcasm, hesitation, or a warm, caring voice.

This mode of understanding and translating has sometimes been referred to as "expansion" (Labov & Fanshel, 1977) because it often results in more words rather than fewer, making it in some ways the opposite of meaning unit summarizing. It is particularly relevant to the analysis of data collected when there is no opportunity to ask for clarification or more detail, such as in open-ended questionnaires (e.g., Helpful Aspects of Therapy [HAT] Form; Elliott et al., 2006) and in transcripts of key points within significant moments of interaction (as in the example from Labott et al., 1992, given earlier). Both kinds of data are likely to be both brief and meaning dense, necessitating a more intensive form of listening and understanding than the meaning unit summary mode allows. In such cases, the process of explication can be challenging, requiring the use of deep empathic immersion as a method of analysis (Wertz, 1983). In the extreme, to understand one informant sentence, the researcher may have to listen to the entire interview and, on returning to the key response, try to put self firmly in the speaker's shoes, asking, "What did they mean there?" "What are they really saying?" and "What is implied or said between the lines?" (Elliott, 1993).

6. Interpreting Nonconscious Meaning

In the first two modes of understanding and translating, the researcher is deliberately trying to capture the participant's conscious meaning; in this sense, it is easy to characterize them as more descriptive forms of understanding. However, those are not the only ways of understanding and translating; it is also possible to read beyond what the participant is likely to be aware of, toward more deeply implicit meanings of which the person is likely not aware. This lack of conscious awareness may be because the meanings are avoided out of discomfort or fear (dynamically unconscious), or they may simply be out of the person's momentary frame of reference (temporarily unaware). However, they may be more general unspoken cultural meanings than personal meanings, such as gender roles or implicit bias toward ethnic minorities. In addition, the description applied to the person's experience or action may be expressed in technical language that is foreign to the person and thus out of their frame of reference (e.g., core emotional pain, unmet needs; O'Brien et al., 2019). In such situations, the person might not recognize the translation as a paraphrase of their experience and might experience the technical description as "news." Such more interpretive understandings that deliberately go beyond conscious awareness require an interpretive theory, such as psychoanalysis, Jungian archetypes, feminist-critical theory, or EFT emotion theory. Interpretive theories provide sets of concepts that guide researchers as they try to understand at a deeper level.

However, interpretation is not the same as speculation, and in becoming more interpretive, the researcher still tries to stick close to the data. The difference is that they are not simply trying to let the data or informant speak for themselves but are instead deliberately applying a set of conceptual tools to listen to meaning units in a different way, one that other listeners using the same conceptual tools would be expected to replicate or at least be able to understand.

For example, Elliott and Schnellbacher (2007) did a study of what they called "interpretive discourse analysis," in which each of the two researchers analyzed a collection of HAT Forms in which clients described in writing the most important moment from first sessions of therapy. Schnellbacher analyzed these client descriptions from an interpersonal perspective, focusing on what they implied about the perceived nature of the therapeutic relation ("relational talk"). For his part, Robert analyzed the same descriptions from an EFT emotion-theory perspective, for what they implied about the clients' experiences of their emotions ("emotion talk"). For example, one client described the most helpful event: "Being able to vent without having anything negative be said."

Schnellbacher (Elliott & Schnellbacher, 2007) produced an understanding and translation of this client description as involving

- an image of therapist-other portrayed as (a) an audience that receives the client's story (someone who is talked to) and (b) an accepter (one who accepts the client and is open and amenable to the client's experience; unconditional positive regard) and

- an image of client-self in a relationship with the therapist portrayed as (a) a recipient of acceptance and respect (one who is accepted and respected; unconditional positive regard) and (b) one who is free to vent without receiving a negative reaction by the other.

In contrast, Robert's reading centered on the client's use of the word "vent" as portraying

- an emotion regulation metaphor using a heat or steam metaphor (Lakoff & Johnson, 1980);

- an emotion-driven action tendency: express, vent, or get emotion out in the open;

- a perceived consequence of emotion expression: a lack of negative interpersonal consequences;

- a folk concept of a problematic emotion process—that in general emotional expression is interpersonally risky, a rule noted by virtue of an exception being remarked on here; and

- folk concepts for helpful emotion processes: (a) "It is helpful to express emotions," "Venting metaphor"; (b) "The therapist's acceptance or non-negative response to emotional expression is helpful."

As we have been saying, all forms of understanding and translating are situated within the implicit assumptions of the researcher's frame of reference; however, in interpreting nonconscious meanings, the researcher's interpretive lens is more pronounced and indeed essential as a tool for understanding the participant's data. This mode of understanding and translating participant meaning thus highlights the general interpretive nature of all qualitative understanding and is particularly consistent with the position we have been taking in this book about the value of acknowledging and making use of theory to help us do more illuminating and useful qualitative research. Nevertheless, all three of the modes of understanding and translating we have described have involved trying to capture the content (meaning) of what the participant is saying. In contrast, the final mode of understanding goes beyond the limitations of focusing entirely on content and moves toward understanding action and manner.

7. Process Description

The distinction between process and content has long been enshrined in the psychotherapy research literature (e.g., Kiesler, 1973) and can be found in the philosophy of language as well (e.g., Searle, 1969). *Content* is what a person says, the topic or their meaning. *Process* is everything else (Elliott, 1991): primarily, what the person does by what they say (speech acts or response modes) and how they say it (manner, style). *Process description* is a mode of understanding and translating a participant's communications (spoken or written) by characterizing the nature of their observable speech acts (e.g., minimizing, playing up; narrative actions) or their manner or style (interpersonal stance, vocal quality, emotional arousal level or tone, nonverbals). In other words, we try to understand the process of their communication rather than its content, what they are doing instead of what they are saying. In a way, this is an extension of the previous mode because process description is often out of the person's focal awareness and commonly uses special or technical language. And of course, because we are going beyond the content of what is being said or observed, we are going to have to be guided by a theory of process, whether this is implicit or explicit.

With process description, we also begin to move away from descriptive-interpretive approaches to qualitative analysis and toward the broad field of discourse analysis, including conversation analysis, which lies outside the focus of this book. Nevertheless, we include process description within our generic descriptive-interpretive approach because our goals for using process description and our way of using it fit with the rest of the approach and is, in our experience, fairly different from, say, conversation analysis, which uses quite different rules of evidence and almost never focuses on categorizing things.

We use process description frequently in our work, especially in studies that use therapy session segments as primary data. In general, a clear give-away is a domain of investigation with the word "process" in the title. For example, in the Timulak and Elliott (2003; see Table 4.2) study, all four domains primarily involve process (client problematic process, client and therapist in-session process, event impact on client). It is also worth noting that some interview studies, such as Timulak et al. (2017), may contain what look like process description domains but instead involve clients being explicitly asked to talk about helpful or unhelpful in-session processes as a topic of conversation (i.e., as content). This is not what we mean by process description.

The following is an example of a microanalytic process description, taken from a study by Elliott et al. (1994). In the key response being studied, the therapist said,

> T22: But- but somehow (1.0) (uh), getting into it here is like a painful thing of, (2.4 sec) is it feeling bad about yourself? is it a kind of you as a sham, you as a (<.5) (p. 453)

The following is part of the process analysis of this response:

> Action: (1) Task: Clarify client's painful reaction to seduction theme; (2) Response Modes: Interpretation with question and reflection

> Style: (1) Gentle; (2) searching; (3) collaborative; (4) persistent

As can be seen in this example, process description is an essential part of qualitative research using recordings of interactions, such as therapy session recordings and transcripts.

Critical reflection plays an important role in all these understanding and translating modes; the researcher or analyst should be aware and reflective of what informs their reading of the data (i.e., any assumptions they may have). This critical reflective process can be facilitated by keeping a reflective journal or writing memos, and so forth (Strauss & Corbin, 1998; Taylor et al., 2015).

CATEGORIZING: CREATING AND WORKING WITH CATEGORIES

Once the researchers delineate domains and meaning units and begin the process of understanding and translating those meaning units within the domains, they encounter the second main form of qualitative analysis: creating and working with categories. We discuss four specific modes of analysis within this broad heading of categorizing: category construction, putting meaning units into categories, characterizing categories, and running integrity checks.

8. Category Construction

Category construction involves a set of intertwined activities: It begins with taking the translation of a meaning unit and making categories out of it. This requires naming or renaming the meaning unit. It continues via a process of constant comparison (Glaser & Strauss, 1967), clustering the meaning units according to similarities, which in turn often leads to renaming, and so on. Category construction also, by necessity, involves reification: making processes and experiences into "things" to get a "handle" on them. The clustering process is thus a process of classification. For instance, the following two meaning units can be clustered according to similarity:

> 1-5: Yeah I'm feeling more confident now. I feel that I don't have to be . . . beat yourself up about things that happen in life.

> 2-2: The more self-confidence I got from coming here I could take and apply it to the family situation. That was probably the most important change.

In the example, the participants in both meaning units talk about an increase in their confidence as a result of the experience they have been through, so the category can be called "increased self-confidence."

Categories Versus Themes

As meaning units are clustered, the researchers start to provide provisional names for these clusters of meaning units with similar meanings. We use the term *categorization* (cf. Hill et al., 1997; Hill et al., 2005) for this process. The provisional names are thus provisional categories. We use the term *categories*, but the name for clusters of meaning units could equally be referred to as "themes," "labels," "abbreviated narratives," and so forth. Given that this is a generic framework, we do not insist on the term "category," although for simplicity, in this text we consistently use this term. Other researchers are free to use another term (e.g., "themes," "labels," "codes") as an equivalent for what we call "category." Also, groups of lower order categories are combined to form higher order categories and *narratives* that capture clusters of similar meaning units (e.g., Timulak & Elliott, 2003; see also the next section). Robert says that he has often been asked what the difference is between categories, codes, themes, and so forth. His answer to this question is, "Isn't it interesting how many words English has for the same thing, and how, if there are different words for the same thing, people will invent distinctions between them?"

The Naming of Categories

The naming of categories becomes a critical process here. The words used to name or categorize the clusters of meanings will also be the words used to represent the findings, the results of the qualitative study. The researchers or analysts have to ensure that this wording both captures the shared meaning contained in the data and conveys this meaning in a manner that resonates with the reader. David Rennie (2012) articulated how the researcher's identification of a concept (category) from a meaning unit (which he called "abduction") is followed by the generation of a plausible wording for the category, which must ultimately resonate with the readers' experience when assessing the category and the examples used in the text. Rennie and Fergus (2006) also stressed the role of the bodily felt sense on the part of the researcher, as well as by the reader, in determining whether the wording used for the category fits their experience; they referred to this as an *embodied category*.

We also stress that clarity regarding the researcher's or analyst's interpretive framework will influence the language used in the provisional and final categories. The language used to name categories (and thus to convey meaning) is not just drawn from the language used by the participants either in interviews or observed interactions (subjectivity and meaning making by the participants), it is also informed by the subjectivity (meaning making) of the researcher or analyst. The subjectivity of the researcher or analyst is here informed by their background and interpretive perspective, which may be declared or undeclared, articulated or unarticulated. We believe these perspectives should be articulated and reflected on to enhance the transparency and credibility of the research. For instance, if in a study of the clients' in-session presentations (e.g., O'Brien et al., 2019), we, as researchers, declare our theoretical framework (e.g., the emotion transformation model as postulated by EFT), the readers will be able to situate our clustering, naming, and interpreting of categories. Or in the example of two meaning units reporting on the clients' increased confidence, we used the category "Increased Inner Confidence" (Timulak et al., 2017). One could argue that the word "inner" slipped in due to the experiential orientation of the analysts who place significance on "inner experiencing."

The wording of categories has to also have other characteristics for it to be successful. There is necessarily an aesthetic or literary aspect to the process. As we have outlined elsewhere, the generation and naming of categories is a craft and an art (Timulak & Elliott, 2019). The catchiness or noncatchiness of categories is often a deal maker or breaker in capturing readers' (and reviewers') interest. The generation of categories thus resembles the process of creating poetry. In a less flattering way, the process can also be described as something like advertising, which in a way it is: trying to persuade readers to buy your study, especially your findings. That is why new researchers often have difficulty with this part of the research process, given that bridging the gap between the data and readers in the field requires also knowing the field. Categories should not only be catchy but also have to ring true, to deliver face validity, so that they build readers' confidence and trust in the study. They also have to illuminate phenomena in a way that broadens the reader's perspective (Timulak & Elliott, 2019). Again, in the example of two meaning units, the wording "Increased Inner Confidence" is short and hopefully catchy but also illuminating that it is an "inner experience" of confidence rather than an outward boasting.

The names for parallel sets of categories (as well as domains) should preferably be symmetrical; that is, they should use the same grammatical form—for instance, if adjectives, then only adjectives; if verbs, then only verbs, if short sentences, then short sentences of roughly the same length, and so forth. An effort should be made to retain a similar level of abstraction across categories (see also Timulak & Elliott, 2019). So, apart from "Increased Inner Confidence," we may have other categories of outcome of EFT for generalized anxiety disorder, such as "Improved Self-Esteem," "Better Self-Understanding," "Being Less Anxious," and so forth (see Timulak et al., 2017).

The 37-Category Problem and the Rule of Four
Categories, as with domains and subdomains, are hierarchically organized so that we can have categories of lower and higher orders (i.e., subcategories and superordinate categories). A common problem in qualitative studies is the unnecessary proliferation of categories, which is a clear violation of Occam's razor (entities should not be multiplied without necessity).

Retaining a large number of categories in a given place in an analysis results in a flat, boring analysis and often indicates the analyst has either gotten bored themselves or has lost hope in their analysis. To deal with this problem, we recommend the *rule of four*, which states that whenever the analyst finds a set of four or more parallel categories in an analysis, they should try to form groupings of them, typically adding another layer in the category hierarchy (these two rules are stated in more pithy fashion in Exhibit 4.3). For instance, Timulak and Lietaer (2001) created a higher order category, "Reservations About Therapeutic Relationship," to group together three related subcategories: "Client Uncertainty About Counselor," "Client Deference Toward Counselor," and "Client Examines Counselor." It is common for there to be as many as four to six hierarchical levels of categories.

Once More With Feeling: Domains Are Not Findings

Categories are initially provisional, but as they stabilize, they become the final categories. They communicate the findings of the study. So, although the domains structure the data and findings, the categories say what those findings are; they are the substantive answers to your research questions. The categories are the findings. This is a crucial issue, so we repeat it again: Time and time again, we have found qualitative researchers conflating what they set out to study (i.e., domains of investigation) with what they found (i.e., categories). (Please do not do this, unless you want to cause us pain.)

As a final example of what we are striving for, Levitt, Surace, et al.'s (2018) study of male gay and queer drag performers' experiences of gender looked at, among other things, developmental processes (a domain of investigation) and found the following main category (which they referred to as a cluster): Childhood gender variance and gay-queer identities often led to family of origin rejection. This main category or cluster, in turn, consisted of three (sub)categories:

> 1.1 Beginning to perform drag via childhood dress, play, and holiday costumes (reported by 9 out of 18 informants); 1.2 Interest in doing drag began in context of professional acting in role as woman ($n = 2$); and 1.3 A common need to rise above biological family and culture of origin shame or rejection but, when acceptance of gender and drag was given, it increased closeness ($n = 17$). (Levitt, Surace, et al., 2018, p. 372)

Categories like these can tell us something about the developmental origins of drag performance so that we come away feeling that we have learned something; they may also help reduce prejudice and misunderstanding, which is an important goal for qualitative research.

9. Putting Meaning Units Into Categories

Sometimes, when we come to a meaning unit, it fits perfectly within an existing category or subcategory. Further, as a qualitative analysis progresses, this happens more and more because the categories gradually stabilize. In other words, we move from category construction to coding data into categories to assigning new meaning units to existing categories without the need to modify those categories. We also stop adding new categories or subcategories. This is what grounded theory calls *saturation*, and it tells us that we are nearing the end of our study. However, it is important to point out that this process is not like traditional nominal scale coding systems, in which observations must be assigned to a set of mutually exclusive, predetermined categories. Instead, putting meaning units into categories is a much more open process for two reasons: First, the researcher adds new categories as they go and modifies existing categories. Second, meaning units can go into more than one category. That is, the categories are not assumed to be exhaustive, nor are they necessarily mutually exclusive. (In grounded theory, this is referred to as "open coding"; Strauss & Corbin, 1998).

10. Running Integrity Checks on the Analysis

After all the meaning units have been put in categories and the system of categories has stabilized, it is time to subject the analysis to a selection of checks or evaluations to make sure that the categories fit the data and are coherent (auditing); that you understand how each category is distributed across the sample, which will help you interpret their meaning within the sample (enumerating categories); that you have not just found what you expected (expectation checking); and perhaps even that other researchers can agree on the categories you have found (consensus).

10a. Auditing
The first and most essential of these integrity checks is conducting an audit of the analysis. Although it is possible (and even advisable) for researchers to self-audit, it is much better to use an independent person, preferably a research supervisor or senior researcher, who is somewhat remote from the analysis. The auditing process involves this independent person carefully reviewing the analysis to provide feedback and/or commentary Exhibit 4.2 describes a strategy for auditing qualitative analyses.

10b. Enumerating or Characterizing Categories
As demonstrated by the example in Table 4.1, we also recommend that researchers indicate how representative the categories are within the sample

EXHIBIT 4.2. How to Audit a Qualitative Analysis

Audit steps and practices

A. Preparation

    1. Locate an auditor. This could be a colleague or research supervisor; merits coauthorship.

    2. Prepare complete analysis for auditing. Outline of all the categories and all the meaning units under each category.

B. Category structure checking. Parallel to fine-tooth combing (see next section)

    1. Make sure the categories have a parallel structure so they look like different aspects, phases, and so forth, of the same thing (e.g., activities, properties, gerunds).

    2. Look for redundant or overlapping categories (these have to be collapsed or reconceptualized).

    3. Check for situations where there are too many categories (i.e., four or more) at the same level and place in the analysis; try to find subgroups and suggest subcategory names.

    4. Check to see if there is a logical order or temporal flow to the categories, out of which a mininarrative or sequence could be constructed to make the analysis more lively or descriptive of some sort of process.

C. Fine-tooth combing:

    1. Read all the meaning units under a particular category carefully. With large meaning units mark (underline or highlight) the parts that fit the category.

    2. Look for bits that do not fit the category because they may belong somewhere else or just do not fit.

    3. Look for subgroups of meaning units under the category that indicate the need to add a layer of subcategories (e.g., two closely related but slightly different kinds of experiences).

    4. Check the category label to make sure it fits your felt sense of the meaning units under it; propose revised language for the category label as needed to make it fit.

    5. If appropriate, elaborate the description of the category to bring out its richness.

D. Tentativeness. Use Track Changes when auditing. The analyst knows their data best, which means the auditor's suggestions are always tentative and simply have to be heard and understood by the researcher.

---

of informants. This gives the reader a sense of whether a particular category is based on multiple reports or only one or a small number of participants' reports. We have often come across qualitative studies that did not indicate how representative categories or themes were within the sample. At times, it seems that researchers are worried that doing so would tip the research into positivism. And yet, although the authors do not state exactly how many participants their categories or themes pertain to, they

TABLE 4.1. Example of Enumeration of Categories: The Unmet Needs Domain

Unmet needs	Number of clients	Enumeration category
To be loved and cared for.	14/14[a]	General
To feel validated and understood.	14/14	General
To feel comforted, supported and protected.	14/14	General
To be more self-accepting.	11/14	Typical
To have own autonomy respected.	7/14	Typical

Note. [a]14/14 denotes that 14 out of 14 clients spoke about this. From "Emotion-Focused Perspective on Generalized Anxiety Disorder: A Qualitative Analysis of Clients' In-Session Presentations," by K. O'Brien, N. O'Keeffe, H. Cullen, A. Durcan, L. Timulak, and J. McElvaney, 2019, *Psychotherapy Research*, 29(4), p. 528 (https://doi.org/10.1080/10503307.2017.1373206). Copyright 2019 by Taylor & Francis. Adapted with permission.

may use words such as "some participants" or "few participants," as if quantifying with words was somehow different from quantifying with numbers (cf. Timulak & Elliott, 2019).

The point of enumerating categories is not to emulate quantitative or positivist research but rather to provide a heuristic that interprets the meaning of the category within the sample, thus providing extra information and contributing to the transparency of the analysis. This does not mean that one is implying that the same proportion of responses would be found in a quantitative design using the same categories and examining how representative they are in the population.

In fact, it can be useful to characterize categories broadly in frequency terms that speak directly to the issue of generalizability; this helps the researcher to interpret the meaning of their categories. (This procedure is used in consensual qualitative research [Hill et al., 1997], but Robert developed it in the late 1980s as part of the generic descriptive-interpretive approach; it represents his response at the time to criticisms from positivist researchers.) There are various ways of doing this, such as the following (e.g., used by McGlenn, 1990):

- We can describe some categories or themes as *general* because they occur in all or almost all of our participants' reports (usually at least 80%). General categories are possible defining features ("essences"), which make the phenomenon what it is and not something else (e.g., insight events in therapy and not awareness events; Elliott et al., 1994).

- Categories reported by at least half of participants can be characterized as *typical* and could therefore be used to tell a story about what a typical person's experience is like.

- *Variant* categories are reported by at least two informants (i.e., they are replicated) but fewer than half, which could make them meaningful variations in the phenomenon.

- Finally, categories that appear in the data of only one informant are referred to as *unique*. All we can say about these is that they establish existence—if, of course, we can document them well enough to demonstrate that they are not flukes or errors of some kind.

The point is not to use this scheme as a rigid structure but rather as a heuristic that can help decide what to emphasize in interpreting the meaning of the categories and writing up the study.

Some studies also report how many meaning units fed into various categories, which is information that may be of potential interest to the readers too; however, given that the borders of meaning units are arbitrarily set and that some participants may be vocal and reiterate the same or similar meaning repeatedly, information on how many participants a category pertains to is of much more value than information on how many meaning units fed into a category. Table 4.1 is an example of a table that provides an overview of the main categories and enumerates each one.

10c. Expectation Checking
Another possible integrity check is to assess the relationship between a qualitative researcher's expectations and the results they have obtained (Elliott, 1989). Originally, this check was developed in response to positivist colleagues who claimed that the results of qualitative studies would inevitably be hopelessly biased by researcher expectations; the procedure thus provides a check against this possibility. However, after two tests (Elliott, 1989; Elliott et al., 1994), it became evident that qualitative research is quite able to refute expectations and uncover unexpected findings. Nowadays, we recommend this check for identifying unexpected categories, which can also be useful for writing up the results of a qualitative study:

1. Optional step: At the beginning of the study or early on, write down your initial expectations for what you think you will find. Put these to one side for now (in a drawer or folder on your computer where you can find them later).

2. At the end of the analysis phase of your study, write down what you now know that you expected ("emergent expectations"). This will be based on your sense of how surprised you were versus how much you expected the category.

3. Next, go through all the themes or categories you found in your analysis, including the ones you found in only one informant's data ("unique themes") and rate them on the following four-point scale: 3, clearly expected; 2, somewhat expected; 1, not expected; 0, clearly surprising. Use these ratings to evaluate the degree to which your obtained results were expected or not, counting 2 and 3 as "expected" and 0 and 1 as "not expected."

4. Now compare your expectations with what you found, counting categories and themes that occurred in at least half of your informants or protocols as "present" and those that occurred in less than half as "nonpresent."

One of the payoffs here is the identification of what the study has discovered—that is, things you found even though you did not expect them. As qualitative researchers, one of our greatest pleasures is being surprised by discovering new things, and this procedure provides a systematic way of identifying these, which in turn, we might want to later emphasize in the write-up of the study.

10d. Optional Checks With Other Researchers

Although not essential, another possible integrity check is taking a consensual approach using multiple researchers analyzing the same data and coming to an agreement among themselves on a single version, as is done in consensual qualitative research (cf. Hill et al., 1997, 2005). This can be quite labor intensive, so it is probably best used when there are plenty of people to help with the analysis. For example, one of our studies (Elliott et al., 1994) used a consensus method with multiple qualitative analysts looking at the same data. In this study, three researchers first analyzed a significant event. Then, after discussing the differences, one researcher drafted a consensus version incorporating as much of the three separate analyses as possible and gave it to the other researcher for correction and further discussion until consensus was reached.

Another possibility is using a quasi-quantitative means of reliability checking—for example, by converting a taxonomy of categories (i.e., findings established by an inductively conducted analysis) into a content analysis system using either a nominal scale or a set of presence-absence rating items, one for each category. This is then used by multiple raters for rating the same data (or a new data set) from which the taxonomy was originally developed (e.g., Elliott et al., 1985; Timulak, 2007). We can then conduct a reliability analysis, such as assessing agreement between raters (using Cohen's kappa or Cronbach's alpha). This can potentially build credibility if it shows that independent raters can rate the data similarly among themselves and potentially similar to the original analysts. Any disagreements here can be inspected and a consensus potentially sought.

INTEGRATING THE FINDINGS

11. Depicting Structure and Providing Summary Narratives

In reality, the findings of a descriptive-interpretive study may take many forms, but we recommend using both visual depictions and verbal summary narratives. Visual or graphic diagrams or flow charts representing categories and the links among them can be useful but must be able to stand on their own, without much help from the main body of text in the study. There is an art to constructing such figures, and we recommend conventions such as the use of arrows (→) to depict linear temporal (before–after) relationships, which may (or may not) be causal (e.g., trigger → global distress), and lines (-- or |) to depict expository (part-whole or hierarchical structures) relationships, which indicate logical relationships (e.g., subtypes of unmet need). Figure 4.1 illustrates a model integrating the general categories from McGlenn (1990) into a temporal sequence model, which also illustrates the role of domain structure in constructing such models.

As we mentioned previously, although we use the term "category" to label clusters of meaning units, they sometimes may take the form of higher order categories that form multiple abbreviated narratives made up of lower order categories. For example, Table 4.2 (from Timulak & Elliott, 2003) shows an example of processes involved in two types of empowerment events in EFT for depression. The point is to tell an interesting, compelling story—or set of stories—from the analysis. This could be a story of a typical instance of the phenomenon or its general features.

SUMMARY OF KEY POINTS: QUALITATIVE RESEARCH "SECRETS"

We conclude this chapter by offering what we hope is a list of useful sayings about qualitative analysis (see Exhibit 4.3). These are things no one told us when we started doing qualitative research. Because we had to learn them the hard way, it felt as though we had gained knowledge of something that had previously been secret. We do not necessarily want to deprive you of the adventure of learning these things for yourself, but we hope that you will find at least some of them useful in your journey into qualitative research.

FIGURE 4.1. General Model of a Significant Weeping Event

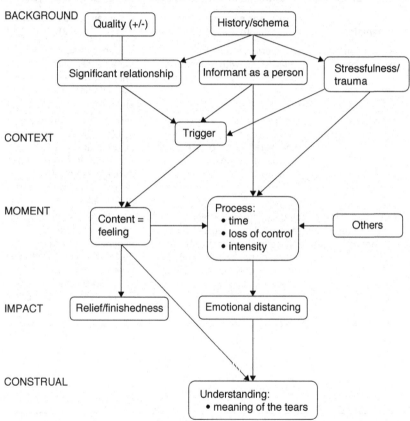

From *A Qualitative Study of Significant Weeping Events* (unpublished doctoral dissertation, p. 72), by M. L. McGlenn, 1990, University of Toledo. Copyright 1990 by M. L. McGlenn. Adapted with permission.

TABLE 4.2. Example of Domains and Integrated Narratives and Ideal Types

Domain	Poignant empowerment (*n* = 3)	Emergent empowerment (*n* = 2)
Client problematic experience	Sad experience concerning a relationship with a significant other (s.o.)	A presence of submerged unexpressed and unacknowledged part of the self containing hurts and blocks
Client process	Describes for the therapist sad or moving (past) experiences connected with a problem in close attachment relationships	Gives voice to a part of the self that plans to enact an action that would help to cope with unresolved hurt in relationship with an s.o. or to a deeply valued part of the self
Therapist process and therapeutic interaction	Being empathically (deeply, humanly) involved, providing space for the client to tell a story, clarifying the client's felt meanings, communicating precise understanding	Facilitates expression of and validates the client's experience of the important part of the self that either bears potential to cope with hurt or that contains deeply valued ideal aspects of the self
Event impact on client	Ambivalent empowerment, awareness of nurturing aspects of attachment-relationships with the s.o., determination to actively cope with aspects of the situation	Feeling highly understood and supported; a stimulation of the client's thinking

Note. From "Empowerment Events in Process-Experiential Psychotherapy of Depression: An Exploratory Qualitative Analysis," by L. Timulak and R. Elliott, 2003, *Psychotherapy Research*, *13*(4), pp. 449–450 (https://doi.org/10.1093/ptr/kpg043). Copyright 2003 by Taylor & Francis. Adapted with permission.

EXHIBIT 4.3. Twelve Secrets About Qualitative Analysis That We Wish Someone Had Told Us

A. On short cuts

1. Selecting the bits you find interesting from a transcript is not qualitative analysis; it is journalism. Qualitative analysis holds itself responsible for all meaning units.

2. Computer software, such as NVIVO or MaxQDA, can be useful for housekeeping (i.e., counting categories, keeping things neat) but does not do qualitative data analysis. Only people can do that.

3. The easiest, cheapest qualitative analysis software is Word, configured with two windows (one for your data, the other for your analysis).

B. On domains versus categories

4. It can be useful to divide your data up into broad, organizing *domains* (e.g., context, event, effects). These generally correspond to your research domains or questions for investigation or interview topics but may evolve as you do your research.

5. A category goes beyond broad, logical headings to tell you something specific about what you are studying, an answer to one of your research questions.

6. Finding "categories" that correspond roughly to your interview schedule questions or domains of investigation is not an analysis. If you stop there, you have wasted everyone's time, including your informants'.

C. On categories

7. Stomach coding. When you read your data, pay attention to how they feel in your chest or gut. When you make a new category or code a piece of data into a new category, make sure your stomach agrees with it. (Thanks to Gendlin by way of Rennie.)

8. The 37-category problem. Avoid the unnecessary multiplication of categories (Occam's razor). Do not let your categories multiply like rabbits until they overrun your analysis. (Also known as the flat, boring analysis problem.)

9. Organize your categories into hierarchies. Some categories are bigger, more abstract, broader, or more important than others. Stack them up like coat hanger trees or organizational charts three, four, five, or even six deep. But do try to resist the temptation to use Word table columns to represent different category levels, which will unnecessarily limit you to two or three levels. Instead, use a numerical outline format (e.g., Category 2.1.3: Helpful client circumstances/situation).

10. Constant comparison. Every time you come to a new meaning unit or add a new category, compare it with all your other meaning units and categories, and then either put it into an existing category or make up a new category for it if it does not fit any place. (This can be tedious at first but becomes easy as your category system develops. Use your stomach to help you.)

11. The rule of four. Whenever you get four or more categories at a particular level in your analysis, look to see how the categories relate to each other:

    - They might go under a higher order category,

    - they might form a sequence or narrative,

    - they might fit on some kind of dimension or continuum,

    - or they might not. But at least check!

12. Make a picture, flow chart, or table that tells a story with your categories. It is a lot more fun that just using words and will force you to think more carefully about how the categories relate to each other to elaborate an experience or tell a story.

5 WRITING THE MANUSCRIPT

Building on the tradition of setting standards for qualitative studies and their write-ups, specifically in psychology (e.g., Elliott et al., 1999), recent developments have seen several efforts to address the issue of standards for reporting qualitative research. First, the Society for Qualitative Inquiry in Psychology (a section of Division 5 of the American Psychological Association [APA]) published its recommendations (Levitt, Motulsky, et al., 2017). This was followed by the recommendations of a task force formed by the APA Publications and Communications Board (Levitt, Bamberg, et al., 2018). Heidi Levitt (2019) summarized these developments in a book on reporting standards for qualitative research for APA publications. We refer the reader to these recent publications because they represent a thorough and detailed account of what should be kept in mind when writing up a qualitative study. They also inform the reader about likely expectations of editors, reviewers, and a critical audience, particularly in the context of APA journals.

We take up how our approach aligns with these methodological integrity standards in Chapter 6. Here, however, we offer a highly selective number of pointers for various aspects of manuscript writing as it pertains to the

https://doi.org/10.1037/0000224-005
Essentials of Descriptive-Interpretive Qualitative Research: A Generic Approach,
by R. Elliott and L. Timulak
Copyright © 2021 by the American Psychological Association. All rights reserved.

characteristics of generic descriptive-interpretive qualitative research (GDI-QR) and that we believe should be addressed in relevant sections of an article. We discuss these pointers under the headings of a typical (APA) journal article: introduction, method, results, discussion. Before we do so, we stress that the overall format of a qualitative paper describing a study conducted following the approach outlined in this book may depend on the type of journal to which the study is submitted and the context of the wider discipline (e.g., gender and sexuality research). Disciplines and journals have their own culture, and there are conventions regarding tone and how papers are pitched and presented. Some journals have many qualitative articles; some have only a few. Previously published articles in a given journal can also create precedents that shape what readers may expect in a report and, therefore, inform what features the report on the study may include. The same applies to the question of discipline. Some disciplines (e.g., psychotherapy research) may be more used to qualitative research, whereas others (e.g., personality psychology) may be less so. It is good for authors to be aware of such factors and attempt to shape a report that bridges possible expectations of the readership. Levitt (2019) provided tips for rhetorical style, given various cultural and contextual factors.

INTRODUCTION

In terms of introduction, we argue that a paper reporting on a qualitative study follows the same logic as any other empirical paper. It is important to establish the relevance of the subject of study, provide a context about what is known in the subject area (based on an extensive review of the literature), and identify what questions remain unanswered. The authors have to articulate a rationale for their study, formulate the research problem, and, if fitting, express it in the form of a research question or questions. If unanswered questions imply the utility of particular modes of inquiry or methodological approaches (e.g., the subject was studied quantitatively, but there remain questions that would be best answered with a qualitative study), the authors might highlight this in the introduction, and the rationale for the study might include an articulation of the need for the particular methodological approach (i.e., descriptive-interpretive qualitative) they are going to use. In theoretically informed studies, when reviewing the existing knowledge, authors may situate their conceptualizations within particular theoretical traditions (e.g., studying clients' experiences in the context of emotion-focused theory).

METHOD

Among the many other things that each qualitative study report should include (e.g., sample characteristics, procedure; see Levitt, 2019; Levitt, Bamberg, et al., 2018), we strongly recommend that the authors be explicit about the conceptual structure they are bringing to study. What domains of investigation were articulated before the study started? What domains of investigation emerged as the study evolved? If the study was theoretically driven, this process may be easier because the theory will most likely have been formulated and articulated in other scholarly writings that can be referenced. If the structure brought by researchers to the study is not based on an explicit theory, the articulation of this structure is harder but is even more important because the reader has to see the steps taken and understand the reasons for those. For instance, it is important to communicate the conceptual basis for formulating interview questions (or domains of observations). The interview questions (domains of observation) do not just "appear"; they are a result of careful considerations and reasoning, and these should be shared with the audience.

In keeping with the established standards (e.g., Levitt, Bamberg, et al., 2018), we strongly advocate that the final interview schedule (or domains of observation in observer-based studies) is explicitly shared in the main body of the article because it is the main data collection tool that the reader or reviewer will critically assess. We have come across too many papers that do not provide information about the interview schedule that was used, how it was constructed, what informed its construction, and what the final or evolving schedule looked like. The result is that we cannot tell how the researcher's conceptual framework may have affected the data obtained and reported.

An explicit articulation of how domains of investigation are constructed, and data collected, should then be matched by an explicit articulation of the interpretive framework used by the researchers and analysts in the data analysis. Again, too many authors are silent on this or simply refer to a brand-name method used or to "bracketing" and "letting the data speak for themselves." Thus, we recommend that authors endeavor to articulate their interpretive framework clearly and that they are as explicit as possible about this in the write-up of the paper. Again, this may be easier to accomplish if that framework is based on an existing, publicly available theoretical conceptualization (e.g., feminist-critical theory). Then, the authors may refer to the existing scholarly work. Alternatively, if the authors do not subscribe to an explicit theoretical framework, they will have to reflect on their implicit personal or theoretical stance and how it may have informed their reading and interpretation of the data. The authors will have to situate themselves as researchers with their own personal and theoretical lenses. This requires not only self-reflection and self-knowledge but also skill in communicating this to readers and reviewers in a way that allows them to both understand and critically evaluate the researchers' interpretations and readings of the data. Again, in our experience, this is all too often missing in qualitative studies.

Thus, we especially wish to stress that in addition to all the other important aspects of reporting on qualitative studies (e.g., situating the sample, rationale behind the sample, clearly articulated procedure of sample recruiting, data collection, data analysis, explanation of various credibility checks; cf. Levitt, 2019; Levitt, Bamberg, et al., 2018), it is crucial to have an explicitly articulated overview of what the researchers brought to the study. That overview might contain what sort of data they were looking for and why (e.g., domains of investigations such as interview schedule, areas of observations, theoretical assumptions, expectations) and how they read and interpreted the data they collected. We stress that simply naming a brand-name approach (e.g., interpretative phenomenological analysis, consensual qualitative research) is not sufficient and does not provide enough information. Instead of general reassurances of objectivity or balance, we want to see a thorough reflection and articulation of where the authors come from and why and how this may have shaped the sort of data obtained and how they were then interpreted. The researcher expectation exercise described in Chapter 4 can help researchers bring out and present their expectations.

RESULTS

As we outlined in Chapter 4—and again, in addition to all those considerations pertaining to the presentation of results and findings stressed in the guidelines mentioned previously (see Levitt, 2019; Levitt, Bamberg, et al., 2018)—we also strongly recommend that the presentation of results clearly distinguish between the structure introduced by the authors and the actual findings. We are deliberate in distinguishing between the two using different terms: domains or subdomains (of investigation) and categories or subcategories (of actual findings).

A perennial issue in qualitative research is managing the space restrictions associated with journal article–length publication. Journal word limits are, in general, a challenge for qualitative researchers, and the descriptive-interpretive genre of qualitative research is no exception. One solution is to focus on the essence of one's findings. We may have to drop a domain from a report altogether or focus only on certain key aspects, sometimes even spreading these out over several publications, as Rennie (1992, 1994a, 1994b, 2007) did with his pivotal work on client in-session experiences. This can pose a dilemma for authors and journal editors because guidelines discouraging piecemeal publication may impose a particular burden for authors writing up complex qualitative studies. Our main advice is for authors to focus on publishing the most important aspects of their studies first and be clear about how a given article differs from previous write-ups drawing on the same data set.

Another strategy for dealing with space limitations is to use visual modes of presentation, such as tables and figures. The general rule is that these have to be understandable on their own. The reader examining a table has to be able to get a sense of what the researchers found without having to dig around in the text. Organizing categories into hierarchies (see Chapter 4) may also be an answer for some studies. The researchers might then focus on more higher order categories with the subcategories being referenced only in passing; at times, more detailed and comprehensive accounts can be provided in online supplements.

We recommend using self-explanatory tables that contain information about how representative findings are of the sample. We also recommend using illustrative quotes that are unambiguous and take the reader through the findings in a way that is easy to follow. We also endorse the use of creative ways to illustrate or summarize findings in the form of figures, pivotal or illustrative cases, and ideal or composite cases (combining results from several cases—see also consensual qualitative research; Hill et al., 2005).

DISCUSSION

The discussion section of a qualitative paper should contain everything that any empirical paper would contain. Situating the findings in the context of previous knowledge, similar studies, and the research questions posed is essential. So, too, is a discussion of implications for future research and theory and, in the case of practical studies, for practice. In terms of limitations and methodological considerations, we stress again the importance of reflecting on the relationship between the authors' conceptualization, how the data were collected, and the interpretive framework used in the analysis. All other typical considerations of limitations are important to report on, such as sample representativeness and generalizability issues, methodological limitations, and suggestions for further research. For more, see Levitt (2019).

KEY POINTS AND EXAMPLES OF GENERIC DESCRIPTIVE-INTERPRETIVE QUALITATIVE RESEARCH STUDIES

As we see it, the challenges of writing up and publishing GDI-QR studies are similar to those facing authors of qualitative research in general. In this chapter, we have described some pointers that we see as more specific to writing up GDI-QR studies, including identifying appropriate journals, providing an appropriate rationale and research questions, describing the domains of investigation and interpretive framework of the researchers, providing the interview or observation protocol, and being specific about the analytic procedures used (along the lines suggested in Chapter 4). We also made recommendations for dealing with the perennial issue of space limitations in presenting findings.

In the Appendix, we offer examples of some GDI-QR studies, where the reader can find good examples of the practices we have highlighted throughout the book. Naturally, we have been selective, offering illustrative examples that represent variations in the method used. The majority of examples are from our field of research, psychotherapy research. However, a large number of quite diverse examples from other disciplines can be easily found. This is because the chapter in which we first described this generic GDI-QR approach (Elliott & Timulak, 2005) has had over 600 citations on Google Scholar, the majority of which are empirical studies using the "method." This means that for further examples, you can go to Google Scholar, search for "Elliott Timulak 2005," and then click on "Cited by."

6

METHODOLOGICAL INTEGRITY

How good is my study? That is the issue behind the jargon term "method-ological integrity." When modern qualitative research methods—especially the descriptive-interpretive approaches we have been presenting—emerged in the 1980s, they were met with a lot of skepticism from quantitative researchers. Traditional quantitative researchers saw these new approaches as second class ways of doing research: at best fit only for doing preliminary pilot studies, at worst as nonresearch or "anecdotal." The only real research used numbers.

As a result, the first generation of qualitative researchers was some-what obsessed with methodological quality. In some cases, this led to the incorporation of methodological procedures based on traditional quantita-tive research, such as the use of multiple qualitative analysts (analogous to interrater reliability), systematic assessment of researcher expectations (analogous to hypothesis testing), and counting the number of respondents who reported a category (analogous to means and standard deviations), procedures we described in Chapters 3 and 4.

https://doi.org/10.1037/0000224-006
Essentials of Descriptive-Interpretive Qualitative Research: A Generic Approach,
by R. Elliott and L. Timulak
Copyright © 2021 by the American Psychological Association. All rights reserved.

It also led to numerous attempts to lay out the methodological guidelines—for example, the Elliott et al. (1999) guidelines, which still represent the primary quality standards for generic descriptive-interpretive qualitative research (GDI-QR). These guidelines, entitled "Evolving Guidelines for Publication of Qualitative Research Studies in Psychology and Related Fields," are divided into two broad headings: general guidelines shared with quantitative research (i.e., explicit scientific context and purpose, appropriate methods, respect for participants, specification of methods, appropriate discussion, clarity of presentation, and contribution to knowledge) and more specific guidelines especially pertinent to GDI-QR (owning one's perspective, situating the sample, grounding in examples, providing credibility checks, coherence, accomplishing general vs. specific research tasks, and resonating with readers). In the meantime, as noted at the beginning of Chapter 5, broader guidelines for conducting and writing up qualitative research have emerged (Levitt, 2019; Levitt, Bamberg, et al., 2018; Levitt, Motulsky, et al., 2017).

Almeida et al. (2019) recently carried out a mapping exercise between the Elliott et al. (1999) guidelines and the more recent American Psychological Association (APA) reporting standards (Levitt, Bamberg, et al., 2018) and found a substantial overlap between them (estimated at 80%). The main difference was the much higher degree of specificity in the APA standards about what has to be reported in write-ups of qualitative studies. However, the Elliott et al. framework offered three additional standards not specifically covered by Levitt, Bamberg, et al. (2018):

> *Respect for participants.* Informed consent, confidentiality, welfare of the participants, social responsibility, and other ethical principles are fulfilled. Researchers creatively adapt their procedures and reports to respect both their participants' lives, and the complexity and ambiguity of the subject matter.
>
> *Clarity of presentation.* The manuscript is well-organized and clearly written, with technical terms defined.
>
> *Resonating with readers.* The manuscript stimulates resonance in readers/ reviewers, meaning that the material is presented in such a way that readers/ reviewers, taking all other guidelines into account, judge it to have represented accurately the subject matter or to have clarified or expanded their appreciation and understanding of it. (pp. 227–229)

Table 6.1 lays out methodological integrity guidelines for GDI-QR and shows their alignment to both the Levitt, Bamberg, et al. (2018) standards and the earlier Elliott et al. (1999) framework in the first two columns of Table 6.1. The right column of the table lays out how methodological integrity is handled in GDI-QR, specifying both the basic expectations of the approach and examples of ideal practice. The basic expectations define

TABLE 6.1. Methodological Integrity Standards in Generic Descriptive-Interpretive Qualitative Research

American Psychological Association Journal Article Reporting Standards (Levitt et al., 2018; abbreviated)	Elliott et al. (1999) publication guidelines (abbreviated)	Implementation in generic descriptive-interpretive qualitative research
1. Assess the adequacy of the data in terms of its ability to capture forms of diversity most relevant to the question, research goals, and inquiry approach.	6. Accomplishing general versus specific research tasks based on an appropriate range of instances (informants or situations) or studied and described systematically and comprehensively enough.	(See Chapter 3.) Basic expectation: Collect enough data (in terms of range and detail) to answer research questions. Ideal practice: In group studies, if possible, collect enough data to achieve saturation.
2. Describe how the researchers' perspectives were managed in both the data collection and analysis (e.g., to limit their effect on the data collection, to structure the analysis).	1. Owning one's perspective: Authors specify their theoretical orientations and personal anticipations, both as known in advance and as they became apparent during the research.	(See Chapters 2 and 4.) Basic expectation: Use critical reflection to examine theoretical commitments and expectations, then disclose these in a report. Ideal practice: Rate categories for how expected these are and look for disconfirming examples that go against expectations.
3. Demonstrate that findings are grounded in the evidence (e.g., using quotes, excerpts).	3. Grounding in examples: Authors provide examples of the data to illustrate the analytic procedures and the understanding developed.	(See Chapter 5.) Basic expectation: Provide one or two well-chosen examples for each category. Ideal practice: Make the complete analysis (all categories with all meaning units) available in a journal supplement or online archive.

(continues)

TABLE 6.1. Methodological Integrity Standards in Generic Descriptive-Interpretive Qualitative Research (Continued)

American Psychological Association Journal Article Reporting Standards (Levitt et al., 2018; abbreviated)	Elliott et al. (1999) publication guidelines (abbreviated)	Implementation in generic descriptive-interpretive qualitative research
4. Demonstrate that the contributions are insightful and meaningful (e.g., in relation to the current literature and the study goal).	6. Accomplishing general versus specific research tasks (see details provided earlier). 7. Resonating with readers: The manuscript stimulates resonance in readers and reviewers; readers and reviewers judge it to have represented accurately the subject matter.	(See Chapter 5.) Basic expectation: Review relevant literature and frame specific research questions in the Introduction, then highlight main findings in the Discussion. Ideal practice: If space permits, present a detailed case study example from data, allowing readers to imagine applying them in practice.
5. Provide relevant contextual information for findings (e.g., setting of study, information about participant, interview question asked is presented before excerpt as needed).	2. Situating the sample: Authors describe the research participants and their life circumstances to aid the reader in judging the range of people and situations to which the findings might be relevant.	(See Chapters 3 and 5.) Basic expectation: Collect and summarize basic demographic data, describe interview protocol and questions. Ideal practice: Provide the entire interview protocol as an appendix or online.
6. Present findings in a coherent manner that makes sense of contradictions or disconfirming evidence in the data (e.g., reconcile discrepancies, describe why a conflict might exist in the findings).	5. Providing coherence: The understanding is represented in a way that achieves coherence and integration while preserving nuances in the data. The understanding fits together to form a data-based story narrative, "map," framework, or underlying structure for the phenomenon or domain.	(See Chapters 4 and 5.) Basic expectation: Provide a summary of structure of main findings in form of verbal text and a table or figure that makes relations among categories clear; note counterinstances. Ideal practice: If possible, find and present an elegant, memorable core structure of the experience that readers can use to retain and apply findings.

7. Demonstrate consistency with regard to the analytic processes or describe responses to inconsistencies.	4. Providing credibility checks: Where relevant, these may include using multiple qualitative analysts, an additional analytic "auditor," or the original analyst for a "verification step" of reviewing the data for discrepancies, overstatements, or errors.	(See Chapters 2 and 4.) Basic expectation: All qualitative analyses are audited by a separate person (e.g., coresearcher or research supervisor). Ideal practice: Two or more researchers independently analyze the data and come up with a consensus version.
8. Describe how support for claims was supplemented by any checks added to the qualitative analysis. Examples of supplemental checks may include triangulation, consensus or auditing, member checks, case examples, structured methods of researcher reflexivity.	4. Providing credibility checks: (a) checking these understandings with the original informants or others similar to them, (b) comparing two or more varied qualitative perspectives, or (c) where appropriate, "triangulation" with external factors (e.g., outcome or recovery) or quantitative data.	(See Chapters 2, 3, and 4.) Basic expectation: Follow a set of systematic and explicit procedures as described in the previous points, including auditing, data displays, examples, and systematic assessment of researcher reflexivity. Ideal practice: Use additional supplemental checks, such as checking transcripts or findings with participants, triangulating with other sources of data, providing detailed case examples.

Note. Adapted from "Journal Article Reporting Standards for Qualitative Primary, Qualitative Meta-Analytic, and Mixed Methods Research in Psychology: The APA Publications and Communications Board Task Force Report," by H. M. Levitt, M. Bamberg, J. W. Creswell, D. M. Frost, R. Josselson, and C. Suárez-Orozco, 2018, *American Psychologist*, 73(1), pp. 36–37 (https://doi.org/10.1037/amp0000151). Copyright 2018 by the American Psychological Association; and from "Evolving Guidelines for Publication of Qualitative Research Studies in Psychology and Related Fields," by R. Elliott, C. T. Fischer, and D. L. Rennie, 1999, *British Journal of Clinical Psychology*, 38(3), p. 228 (https://doi.org/10.1348/014466599162782). Guidelines copyright 1998 by R. Elliott, C. Fischer, and D. Rennie. Adapted with permission.

the backbone of GDI-QR, the standards we think most researchers within this range of approaches will want to adhere to. If you are planning a study within this tradition of qualitative research, you can start with these. In addition, in Table 6.1, for each of the eight rows, we offer suggestions about ideal practice, which significantly exceeds the basic expectations. Largely because of practical circumstances (mostly lack of time or sample limitations), these are not always possible. Think of these as opportunities for "extra credit" that will particularly impress supervisors or reviewers—in the words of Bob Dylan (1965), "to win friends and influence [your] uncle."

Methodological integrity frameworks like the two discussed here have several uses, but their main utility is helping you plan your research. When designing a study, it is useful to run through the list and use it to help you think about what you can do to beef up your study. It is a lot easier to build method safeguards in at the beginning than to try to retrofit them afterward, as we noted in Chapter 2. Finally, they do have another use: to help you write your discussion section, where they provide a helpful structure for identifying the limitations of your study and making recommendations for future research. Methodological integrity guidelines—don't leave home without them to guide you on your research journey!

7
SUMMARY AND CONCLUSIONS

In the previous chapters, we presented principles for following a generic approach to descriptive-interpretive qualitative research (GDI-QR). Given that we encourage creativity and adjusting the procedures to the research problem at hand, we outlined general principles and provided tips based on our experience rather than specifying stringent protocols. At the same time, we are aware of some limitations or caveats. We conclude with a list of hard-won lessons about qualitative research that are incorporated in GDI-QR.

MAIN STRENGTHS OF GDI-QR

Breadth and Flexibility

The main advantage of our formulation is its broad use, flexibility, and creativity. The approach appears to be widely usable and applicable to a range of issues and compatible with many different theoretical perspectives

https://doi.org/10.1037/0000224-007
Essentials of Descriptive-Interpretive Qualitative Research: A Generic Approach,
by R. Elliott and L. Timulak
Copyright © 2021 by the American Psychological Association. All rights reserved.

in psychology, ranging from humanistic to psychodynamic to multicultural. Indeed, studies referencing our original paper (Elliott & Timulak, 2005) extend well beyond psychology. Thus, we hope the more detailed principles we have laid out here can offer a good reference point and guide for researchers who want to approach their area of investigation creatively and flexibly. The principles outlined by us stress scholarly work and rigor, but apart from addressing issues encountered when conducting qualitative research that requires description and interpretation and whose goal is to create categories or themes, they do not set many limits. They allow for various ways of collecting data. And although the principles for data analysis that we outline may appear more prescriptive, they are rather intended as examples of how it can be done rather than as the only way data should be analyzed. The method can be and has been used for case studies, self-report–based studies, observation-based studies, and (although not covered here) qualitative meta-analyses.

Precision in Describing Analysis Procedures

Balancing the flexibility of our generic approach is the high degree to which we have been able to specify the exact activities of the researcher, breaking them down into 11 analysis modes (see Chapter 4). We hope this will provide researchers with the needed structure for planning, carrying out, and writing up their research.

Clarity About the Role of Theory

One area where we perhaps put more emphasis than qualitative methodological formulations typically do is the requirement of a clear articulation of the theoretical and personal perspective brought by researchers. By specifying a clear but delimited role for theory, GDI-QR addresses an issue that qualitative researchers have often struggled with or been confused about.

Clarity About the Difference Between Domains and Categories

We have also provided clear guidance that should enable researchers to avoid a common problem in reporting qualitative studies, by helping them differentiate between the structure that the researchers bring to the research (domains of investigation) and the actual findings (categories, themes, narratives). This is an issue that is often neglected in qualitative research.

LIMITATIONS OF GDI-QR

Lack of Specificity

The main limitation of the approach presented here is the same as its main strength: its broad use, flexibility, and creativity. We worry that we have offered too many options, leaving some readers (especially early career researchers) overwhelmed with a sense of too much freedom and hungry for more specific guidance. We can certainly empathize with this anxiety; we have felt it ourselves often in confronting the seemingly limitless possibilities of qualitative research. We can imagine these readers saying, "Okay, that sounds great, but can't you be more specific? Where do I start?" However, we have tried to be as specific as possible along the way, so in response, we can only gravely quote the King of Hearts from *Alice's Adventures in Wonderland*: "Begin at the beginning and go on till you come to the end: then stop" (Carroll, 1865/2020, p. 173).

Nothing New Here

We imagine that other, perhaps more experienced, readers will say instead that there is little new here that has not already been said by others. However, that is rather the point of a generic approach: to identify what is useful from a collection of different approaches and offer it in an inviting, no-nonsense presentation. We hope we have succeeded at least partially in this. At this point, we could also quote Andre Gide (1891): Everything that needs to be said has already been said. But since no one was listening, everything must be said again.

Another Brand Name

Finally, there is the risk that our generic, descriptive-interpretive formulation could become a brand-name approach in itself. Once there is a clear how-to manual for qualitative research, there is a risk that this may happen. Indeed, we have come across some papers referring to our work as a brand-named approach: the "descriptive-interpretive" method. Although this is a flattering prospect, it is not in our heart of hearts what we want for our readers. Although we cannot control how other authors might use this book to brand what they do, what we want is for them to do their most creative, rigorous best, to tell readers what preunderstandings shaped their research and what specific procedures they followed—and have fun doing it.

IN PARTING: HARD-WON LESSONS

To conclude, we leave you with a list of things we have learned from our more than half-century of combined experience doing qualitative research, lessons that incorporated the approach we presented here. Exhibit 7.1 lists these points, which we have stated strongly and sometimes provocatively for effect. We accept that not everyone will agree with them, but we offer them here because they are the guiding insights that have directed our practice as qualitative researchers and led to the writing of this book.

EXHIBIT 7.1. Parting Shot: Hard-Won Lessons About Qualitative Research in General

---

On how hard it is

- Qualitative research is harder (i.e., more work and more personally challenging) than quantitative research.

- Qualitative research asks more of you as a person because you are the data collection and analysis instrument. A qualitative study will succeed or fail on the basis of your empathic listening skills, your ability to imaginatively enter the informant's world, your ability to put subtle complicated experiences into words, and even how logical you can be and your organizational skills. This is terrifying.

- Because of how hard it is, qualitative research can feel lonely. For that reason, it is nice to do it in groups, but to do that, you have to be a good listener and be willing to see things from other peoples' points of view.

On research questions

- A clear definition of your topic and a clear statement of your research question are the most important requirements of a good qualitative study; it is more important than the specific method you use.

- Qualitative research is good at answering open (exploratory, discovery-oriented) research questions. Conversely, if your main research question is closed (confirmatory, hypothesis testing), you should be doing a quantitative study instead.

Diversity and sameness

- No one does qualitative research in exactly the same way. This is good.

- The brand-name problem: Brand names for qualitative research are social fictions. Empirical phenomenology, interpretative phenomenological analysis, grounded theory analysis, comprehensive process analysis, consensual qualitative research, framework analysis, and thematic analysis are all more similar than they are different. In fact, they do not refer to different methods but rather point to different social networks ("invisible colleges") of qualitative researchers, each with its own local culture and traditions. They are more like dialects than different languages.

EXHIBIT 7.1. Parting Shot: Hard-Won Lessons About Qualitative Research in General (*Continued*)

- The basis for most qualitative research in the social and health sciences today is a general set of research activities (which we have described), at the center of which are researchers' attempts to describe accurately and explain cogently important human experiences or actions.

- On the need to demystify specific qualitative research brand names: To illustrate this point, we will pick on grounded theory analysis (GTA): Although it is the source of most contemporary systematic qualitative research in the social and health sciences, Glaser and Strauss (1967) only described GTA generally. Most of what is called GTA in psychological research today is based on Rennie, Elliott, McLeod, Charmaz (2006), and others' constructions of what they thought Glaser and Strauss (and later Corbin) were talking about.

Appendix

EXEMPLAR STUDIES

The following is an annotated list of examples of generic descriptive-interpretive qualitative (GDI-QR) studies.

Doherty, S., Hannigan, B., & Campbell, M. J. (2016). The experience of depression during the careers of elite male athletes. *Frontiers in Psychology, 7,* 1069. https://doi.org/10.3389/fpsyg.2016.01069
[Straightforward GDI-QR interview study]

L'Estrange, K., Timulak, L., Kinsella, L., & D'Alton, P. (2016). Experiences of changes in self-compassion following mindfulness-based intervention with a cancer population. *Mindfulness, 7*(3), 734–744. https://doi.org/10.1007/s12671-016-0513-0
[Straightforward GDI-QR interview study]

Levitt, H. M., Surace, F. I., Wheeler, E. E., Maki, E., Alcántara, D., Cadet, M., Cullipher, S., Desai, S., Sada, G. G., Hite, J., Kosterina, E., Krill, S., Lui, C., Manove, E., Martin, R. J., & Ngai, C. (2018). Drag gender: Experiences of gender for gay and queer men who perform drag. *Sex Roles, 78*(5–6), 367–384. https://doi.org/10.1007/s11199-017-0802-7
[An example of grounded theory analysis fitting the descriptions of GDI-QR]

O'Brien, K., O'Keeffe, N., Cullen, H., Durcan, A., Timulak, L., & McElvaney, J. (2019). Emotion-focused perspective on generalised anxiety disorder: A qualitative analysis of clients' in-session presentations. *Psychotherapy Research, 29*(4), 524–540. https://doi.org/10.1080/10503307.2017.1373206
[Theoretically informed analysis]

Richards, D., & Timulak, L. (2012). Client-identified helpful and hindering events in therapist-delivered vs. self-administered online cognitive-behavioural treatments for depression in college students. *Counselling Psychology Quarterly, 25*(3), 251–262. https://doi.org/10.1080/09515070.2012.703129
[Study using written questionnaires as a means of data collection]

Timulak, L., & Elliott, R. (2003). Empowerment events in process-experiential psychotherapy of depression: An exploratory qualitative analysis. *Psychotherapy Research, 13*(4), 443–460. https://doi.org/10.1093/ptr/kpg043 [Use of narrative-type higher order categories]

References

Almeida, S. N., Elliott, R., Silva, E. R., & Sales, C. M. D. (2019). Fear of cancer recurrence: A qualitative systematic review and meta-synthesis of patients' experiences. *Clinical Psychology Review, 68*, 13–24. https://doi.org/10.1016/j.cpr.2018.12.001

American Psychological Association. (2017). *Ethical principles of psychologists and code of conduct* (2002, Amended June 1, 2010 and January 1, 2017). Retrieved from http://www.apa.org/ethics/code/index.aspx

Baldick, C. (2008). *The Oxford dictionary of literary terms.* Oxford University Press.

Barker, C., Pistrang, N., & Elliott, R. (2015). *Research methods in clinical psychology: An introduction for students and practitioners* (3rd ed.). Wiley. https://doi.org/10.1002/9781119154082

Bhaskar, R. (1978). *A realist theory of science.* Humanities Press.

Braun, V., & Clarke, V. (2006). Using thematic analysis in psychology. *Qualitative Research in Psychology, 3*(2), 77–101. https://doi.org/10.1191/1478088706qp063oa

Brien, C., O'Connor, J., & Russell-Carroll, D. (2018). "Meaningless carrying-on": A psychoanalytically oriented qualitative study of compulsive hoarding. *Psychoanalytic Psychology, 35*(2), 270–279. https://doi.org/10.1037/pap0000100

Brinkmann, S., & Kvale, S. (2018). *Doing interviews* (2nd ed.). SAGE. https://doi.org/10.4135/9781529716665

British Psychological Society. (2018). *Data protection regulation: Guidance for researchers.* https://www.bps.org.uk/news-and-policy/data-protection-regulation-guidance-researchers

Carroll, L. (2020). *Alice's adventures in Wonderland.* http://www.gutenberg.org/ebooks/11 (Original work published 1865)

Charmaz, K. (2006). *Constructing grounded theory: A practical guide through qualitative analysis.* SAGE.

Cook, T. D., & Campbell, D. T. (1979). *Quasi-experimentation: Design and analysis issues for field settings*. Rand McNally.

Davidson, L. (2003). *Living outside mental illness: Qualitative studies of recovery in schizophrenia*. New York University Press.

Denzin, N. K., & Lincoln, Y. S. (Eds.). (1994). *Handbook of qualitative research*. SAGE.

Elliott, R. (1977). *Help-intended-acts* [Unpublished manuscript]. Department of Psychology, University of California, Los Angeles.

Elliott, R. (1983). "That in your hands": A comprehensive process analysis of a significant event in psychotherapy. *Psychiatry, 46*(2), 113–129. https://doi.org/10.1080/00332747.1983.11024185

Elliott, R. (1984). A discovery-oriented approach to significant events in psychotherapy: Interpersonal process recall and comprehensive process analysis. In L. Rice & L. Greenberg (Eds.), *Patterns of change* (pp. 249–286). Guilford Press.

Elliott, R. (1985). Helpful and nonhelpful events in brief counseling interviews: An empirical taxonomy. *Journal of Counseling Psychology, 32*(3), 307–322. https://doi.org/10.1037/0022-0167.32.3.307

Elliott, R. (1986). Interpersonal process recall (IPR) as a psychotherapy process research method. In L. S. Greenberg & W. M. Pinsof (Eds.), *The psychotherapeutic process: A research handbook* (pp. 503–527). Guilford Press.

Elliott, R. (1989). Comprehensive process analysis: Understanding the change process in significant therapy events. In M. Packer & R. B. Addison (Eds.), *Entering the circle: Hermeneutic investigation in psychology* (pp. 165–184). SUNY Press.

Elliott, R. (1991). Five dimensions of therapy process. *Psychotherapy Research, 1*(2), 92–103. https://doi.org/10.1080/10503309112331335521

Elliott, R. (1993). *Comprehensive process analysis: Mapping the change process in psychotherapy* [Unpublished manuscript]. Department of Psychology, University of Toledo.

Elliott, R. (1995). Therapy process research and clinical practice: Practical strategies. In M. Aveline & D. A. Shapiro (Eds.), *Research foundations for psychotherapy practice* (pp. 49–72). Wiley.

Elliott, R. (2008). *Client Change Interview Schedule: Version 5* [Unpublished interview schedule]. Counselling Unit, University of Strathclyde.

Elliott, R., & Anderson, C. (1994). Simplicity and complexity in psychotherapy research. In R. L. Russell (Ed.), *Reassessing psychotherapy research* (pp. 65–113). Guilford Press.

Elliott, R., Fischer, C. T., & Rennie, D. L. (1999). Evolving guidelines for publication of qualitative research studies in psychology and related fields. *British Journal of Clinical Psychology, 38*(3), 215–229. https://doi.org/10.1348/014466599162782

Elliott, R., & Greenberg, L. S. (1997). Multiple voices in process-experiential therapy: Dialogues between aspects of the self. *Journal of Psychotherapy Integration, 7*(3), 225–239. https://doi.org/10.1037/h0101127

Elliott, R., James, E., Reimschuessel, C., Cislo, D., & Sack, N. (1985). Significant events and the analysis of immediate therapeutic impacts. *Psychotherapy: Theory, Research, & Practice, 22*(3), 620–630. https://doi.org/10.1037/h0085548

Elliott, R., & Schnellbacher, J. (2007, June 20–23). *Relational and emotion processes in first sessions of process-experiential therapy: An interpretive discourse analysis of clients' accounts of significant events* [Paper presentation]. Society for Psychotherapy Research, Madison, WI, United States.

Elliott, R., & Shapiro, D. A. (1988). Brief structured recall: A more efficient method for studying significant therapy events. *The British Journal of Medical Psychology, 61*(2), 141–153. https://doi.org/10.1111/j.2044-8341.1988.tb02773.x

Elliott, R., & Shapiro, D. A. (1992). Clients and therapists as analysts of significant events. In S. G. Toukmanian & D. L. Rennie (Eds.), *Two perspectives on psychotherapeutic change: Theory-guided and phenomenological research strategies* (pp. 163–186). SAGE.

Elliott, R., Shapiro, D. A., Firth-Cozens, J., Stiles, W. B., Hardy, G. E., Llewelyn, S. P., & Margison, F. R. (1994). Comprehensive process analysis of insight events in cognitive-behavioral and psychodynamic-interpersonal psychotherapies. *Journal of Counseling Psychology, 41*(4), 449–463. https://doi.org/10.1037/0022-0167.41.4.449

Elliott, R., Slatick, E., & Urman, M. (2006). Qualitative change process research on psychotherapy: Alternative strategies. In J. Frommer & D. L. Rennie (Eds.), *Qualitative psychotherapy research: Methods and methodology* (pp. 69–111). Pabst Science Publishers.

Elliott, R., & Timulak, L. (2005). Descriptive and interpretive approaches to qualitative research. In J. Miles & P. Gilbert (Eds.), *A handbook of research methods in clinical and health psychology* (pp. 147–159). Oxford University Press.

Elliott, R., Watson, J., Goldman, R. N., & Greenberg, L. S. (2004). *Learning emotion-focused therapy: The process-experiential approach to change.* American Psychological Association. https://doi.org/10.1037/10725-000

Emerson, R., Fretz, R., & Shaw, L. L. (2011). *Writing ethnographic fieldnotes* (2nd ed.). University of Chicago Press. https://doi.org/10.7208/chicago/9780226206868.001.0001

Etherington, K. (2004). *Becoming a reflexive researcher—using our selves in research.* Jessica Kingsley.

Feyerabend, P. (1975). *Against method.* Verso.

Gide, A. (1891). *Le traité du Narcisse: Théorie du symbole* [The treatise of Narcissus: Theory of the symbol]. Librairie de l'Art Indépendant.

Giorgi, A. (1975). An application of phenomenological method in psychology. In A. Giorgi, C. Fisher, & E. Murray (Eds.), *Duquesne studies in phenomenological psychology* (Vol. 2, pp. 23–85). Duquesne University Press. https://doi.org/10.5840/dspp197529

Giorgi, A. (1985). Sketch of a psychological phenomenological method. In A. Giorgi (Ed.), *Phenomenology and psychological research* (pp. 8–22). Duquesne University Press.

Glaser, B. G. (1978). *Theoretical sensitivity*. Sociology Press.

Glaser, B. G., & Strauss, A. L. (1967). *The discovery of grounded theory: Strategies for qualitative research*. Aldine.

Greenberg, L. S., & Pascual-Leone, J. (1995). A dialectical constructivist approach to experiential change. In R. Neimeyer & M. Mahoney (Eds.), *Constructivism in psychotherapy* (pp. 169–191). American Psychological Association. https://doi.org/10.1037/10170-008

Guest, G. S., Namey, E. E., & Mitchell, M. L. (2013). *Collecting qualitative data: A field manual for applied research*. SAGE. https://doi.org/10.4135/9781506374680

Heidegger, M. (1962). *Being and time* (J. Macquarrie & E. Robinson, Trans.). Harper & Row.

Hill, C. E. (1974). A comparison of the perceptions of a therapy session by clients, therapists and objective judges. *JSAS Catalog of Selected Documents in Psychology, 4*, 16 (Ms. No. 564).

Hill, C. E. (Ed.). (2012). *Consensual qualitative research: A practical resource for investigating social science phenomena*. American Psychological Association.

Hill, C. E., Knox, S., Thompson, B. J., Williams, E. N., Hess, S. A., & Ladany, N. (2005). Consensual qualitative research: An update. *Journal of Counseling Psychology, 52*(2), 196–205. https://doi.org/10.1037/0022-0167.52.2.196

Hill, C. E., Thompson, B. J., & Williams, E. N. (1997). A guide to conducting consensual qualitative research. *The Counseling Psychologist, 25*(4), 517–572. https://doi.org/10.1177/0011000097254001

Hissa, J., & Timulak, L. (2020). Theoretically-informed qualitative research in psychotherapy [Special issue]. *Counselling and Psychotherapy Research*. Advance online publication. https://doi.org/10.1002/capr.12301

Iphofen, R., & Tolich, M. (Eds.). (2018). *The SAGE handbook of qualitative research ethics*. SAGE. https://doi.org/10.4135/9781526435446

Kagan, N. (1975). *Interpersonal process recall: A method of influencing human interaction* [Unpublished manuscript]. Office of Medical Education, Michigan State University.

Kiesler, D. J. (1973). *The process of psychotherapy*. Aldine.

Klein, M. J., & Elliott, J. (2006). Client accounts of personal change in process-experiential psychotherapy: A methodologically pluralistic approach. *Psychotherapy Research, 16*(1), 91–105. https://doi.org/10.1080/10503300500090993

Knox, S., & Burkard, A. W. (2009). Qualitative research interviews. *Psychotherapy Research, 19*(4–5), 566–575. https://doi.org/10.1080/10503300802702105

Krueger, R. A., & Casey, M. A. (2014). *Focus groups: A practical guide for applied research* (5th ed.). SAGE.

Kvale, S. (1996). *InterViews: An introduction to qualitative research interviewing*. SAGE.

Labott, S. M., Elliott, R., & Eason, P. S. (1992). "If you love someone, you don't hurt them": A comprehensive process analysis of a weeping event in therapy. *Psychiatry, 55*(1), 49–62. https://doi.org/10.1080/00332747.1992.11024579

Labov, W., & Fanshel, D. (1977). *Therapeutic discourse*. Academic Press.

Ladany, N., Thompson, B. J., & Hill, C. E. (2012). Cross-analysis. In C. E. Hill (Ed.), *Consensual qualitative research: A practical resource for investigating social science phenomena* (pp. 117–134). American Psychological Association.

Lakoff, G., & Johnson, M. (1980). *Metaphors we live by*. University of Chicago Press.

Lather, P. (1991). *Getting smart: Feminist research and pedagogy with/in the postmodern*. Routledge. https://doi.org/10.4324/9780203451311

L'Estrange, K., Timulak, L., Kinsella, L., & D'Alton, P. (2016). Experiences of changes in self-compassion following mindfulness-based intervention with a cancer population. *Mindfulness, 7*(3), 734–744. https://doi.org/10.1007/s12671-016-0513-0

Levitt, H. M. (2019). *Reporting qualitative research in psychology: How to meet APA Style journal article reporting standards*. American Psychological Association. https://doi.org/10.1037/0000121-000

Levitt, H. M., Bamberg, M., Creswell, J. W., Frost, D. M., Josselson, R., & Suárez-Orozco, C. (2018). Journal article reporting standards for qualitative primary, qualitative meta-analytic, and mixed methods research in psychology: The APA Publications and Communications Board task force report. *American Psychologist, 73*(1), 26–46. https://doi.org/10.1037/amp0000151

Levitt, H. M., Motulsky, S. L., Wertz, F. J., Morrow, S. L., & Ponterotto, J. G. (2017). Recommendations for designing and reviewing qualitative research in psychology: Promoting methodological integrity. *Qualitative Psychology, 4*(1), 2–22. https://doi.org/10.1037/qup0000082

Levitt, H. M., Pomerville, A., Surace, F. I., & Grabowski, L. M. (2017). Meta-method study of qualitative psychotherapy research on clients' experiences: Review and recommendations. *Journal of Counseling Psychology, 64*(6), 626–644. https://doi.org/10.1037/cou0000222

Levitt, H. M., Surace, F. I., Wheeler, E. E., Maki, E., Alcántara, D., Cadet, M., Cullipher, S., Desai, S., Sada, G. G., Hite, J., Kosterina, E., Krill, S., Lui, C., Manove, E., Martin, R. J., & Ngal, C. (2018). Drag gender: Experiences of gender for gay and queer men who perform drag. *Sex Roles, 78*(5–6), 367–384. https://doi.org/10.1007/s11199-017-0802-7

Llewelyn, S. P. (1988). Psychological therapy as viewed by clients and therapists. *British Journal of Clinical Psychology, 27*(3), 223–237. https://doi.org/10.1111/j.2044-8260.1988.tb00779.x

Mahrer, A. R. (1988). Discovery-oriented psychotherapy research: Rationale, aims, and methods. *American Psychologist, 43*(9), 694–702. https://doi.org/10.1037/0003-066X.43.9.694

McElvaney, J., & Timulak, L. (2013). Clients' experience of therapy and its outcomes in quantitatively "good outcome" and "poor outcome" psychological therapy in a primary care setting. *Counselling & Psychotherapy Research, 13,* 246–253. https://doi.org/10.1080/14733145.2012.761258

McGlenn, M. L. (1990). *A qualitative study of significant weeping events* [Unpublished doctoral dissertation]. University of Toledo.

McLeod, J. (2001). *Qualitative research in counselling and psychotherapy.* SAGE. https://doi.org/10.4135/9781849209663

McLeod, J. (2011). *Qualitative research in counselling and psychotherapy* (2nd ed.). SAGE.

O'Brien, K., O'Keeffe, N., Cullen, H., Durcan, A., Timulak, L., & McElvaney, J. (2019). Emotion-focused perspective on generalized anxiety disorder: A qualitative analysis of clients' in-session presentations. *Psychotherapy Research, 29*(4), 524–540. https://doi.org/10.1080/10503307.2017.1373206

Packer, M. J., & Addison, R. B. (Eds.). (1989). *Entering the circle: Hermeneutic investigation in psychology.* SUNY Press.

Pascual-Leone, J. (1991). Emotions, development, and psychotherapy: A dialectical-constructivist perspective. In J. D. Safran & L. S. Greenberg (Eds.), *Emotion, psychotherapy, and change* (pp. 302–335). Guilford Press.

Patton, M. Q. (2015). *Qualitative evaluation and research methods* (4th ed.). SAGE.

Piaget, J. (1970). *Structuralism.* Harper & Row.

Polkinghorne, D. (1983). *Methodology for the human sciences.* SUNY Press.

Ponterotto, J. G. (2005). Qualitative research in counseling psychology: A primer on research paradigms and philosophy of science. *Journal of Counseling Psychology, 52*(2), 126–136. https://doi.org/10.1037/0022-0167.52.2.126

Popper, K. (1959). *The logic of scientific discovery.* Basic Books.

Rees, A., Hardy, G. E., Barkham, M., Elliott, R., Smith, J. A., & Reynolds, S. (2001). 'It's like catching a desire before it flies away': A comprehensive process analysis of a problem clarification event in cognitive-behavioral therapy for depression. *Psychotherapy Research, 11*(3), 331–351. https://doi.org/10.1080/713663987

Rennie, D. L. (1990). Toward a representation of the client's experience of the psychotherapy hour. In G. Lietaer, J. Rombauts, & R. Van Balen (Eds.), *Client-centered and experiential psychotherapy towards the nineties* (pp. 155–172). Leuven University Press.

Rennie, D. L. (1992). Qualitative analysis of the client's experience of psychotherapy: The unfolding of reflexivity. In S. Toukmanian & D. L. Rennie (Eds.), *Psychotherapy process research: Paradigmatic and narrative approaches* (pp. 211–233). SAGE.

Rennie, D. L. (1994a). Client's deference in psychotherapy. *Journal of Counseling Psychology, 41*(4), 427–437. https://doi.org/10.1037/0022-0167.41.4.427

Rennie, D. L. (1994b). Storytelling in psychotherapy: The client's subjective experience. *Psychotherapy: Theory, Research, & Practice, 31*(2), 234–243. https://doi.org/10.1037/h0090224

Rennie, D. L. (1998). Forging a methodical way between objectivism and relativism. [Review of the books *InterViews*, by S. Kvale, and *Psychological research*, by J. Haworth, Ed.]. *Theory & Psychology, 8*(4), 575–576. https://doi.org/10.1177/0959354398084009

Rennie, D. L. (2007). Clients' accounts of resistance in counselling: A qualitative analysis. *Canadian Journal of Counselling and Psychotherapy, 28*(1). https://cjc-rcc.ucalgary.ca/article/view/58492

Rennie, D. L. (2012). Qualitative research as methodical hermeneutics. *Psychological Methods, 17*(3), 385–398. https://doi.org/10.1037/a0029250

Rennie, D. L., & Fergus, K. D. (2006). Embodied categorizing in the grounded theory method: Methodical hermeneutics in action. *Theory & Psychology, 16*(4), 483–503. https://doi.org/10.1177/0959354306066202

Rennie, D. L., Phillips, J. R., & Quartaro, G. K. (1988). Grounded theory: A promising approach to conceptualization in psychology? *Canadian Psychology, 29*(2), 139–150. https://doi.org/10.1037/h0079765

Rhodes, R. H., Hill, C. E., Thompson, B. J., & Elliott, R. (1994). Client retrospective recall of resolved and unresolved misunderstanding events. *Journal of Counseling Psychology, 41*(4), 473–483. https://doi.org/10.1037/0022-0167.41.4.473

Richards, D., & Timulak, L. (2012). Client-identified helpful and hindering events in therapist-delivered vs. self-administered online cognitive-behavioural treatments for depression in college students. *Counselling Psychology Quarterly, 25*(3), 251–262. https://doi.org/10.1080/09515070.2012.703129

Rober, P., Elliott, R., Buysse, A., Loots, G., & De Corte, K. (2008). What's on the therapist's mind? A grounded theory analysis of family therapist reflections during individual therapy sessions. *Psychotherapy Research, 18*(1), 48–57. https://doi.org/10.1080/10503300701324183

Runyan, W. M. (1982). *Life histories and psychobiography: Explorations in theory and method.* Oxford University Press.

Sacks, H., Schegloff, E. A., & Jefferson, G. (1974). A simplest systematics for the organization of turn-taking in conversation. *Language, 50*(4), 696–735. https://doi.org/10.1353/lan.1974.0010

Searle, J. R. (1969). *Speech acts: An essay in the philosophy of language.* Cambridge University Press. https://doi.org/10.1017/CBO9781139173438

Siegfried, T. (2010, March 27). Odds are, it's wrong: Science fails to face the shortcomings of statistics. *Science News, 177*(7), 26–29. https://doi.org/10.1002/scin.5591770721

Sim, W., Huang, T. C., & Hill, C. E. (2012). Biases and expectations. In C. E. Hill (Ed.), *Consensual qualitative research: A practical resource for investigating social science phenomena* (pp. 59–70). American Psychological Association.

Smith, J. A., Flowers, P., & Larkin, M. (2009). *Interpretative phenomenological analysis: Theory, method and research.* SAGE.

Stewart, D. W., & Shamdasani, P. N. (2014). *Focus groups: Theory and practice* (3rd ed.). SAGE.

Stiles, W. B. (1986). Levels of intended meaning of utterances. *British Journal of Clinical Psychology, 25*(3), 213–222. https://doi.org/10.1111/j.2044-8260.1986.tb00697.x

Stiles, W. B. (2003). Qualitative research: Evaluating the process and the product. In S. Llewelyn & P. Kennedy (Eds.), *Handbook of clinical health psychology* (pp. 477–499). Wiley. https://doi.org/10.1002/0470013389.ch24

Stiles, W. B. (2015). Theory building, enriching, and fact gathering: Alternative purposes of psychotherapy research. In O. Gelo, A. Pritz, & B. Rieken (Eds.), *Psychotherapy research* (pp. 159–179). Springer. https://doi.org/10.1007/978-3-7091-1382-0_8

Strauss, A., & Corbin, J. (1998). *Basics of qualitative research: Techniques and procedures for developing grounded theory* (2nd ed.). SAGE.

Tashakkori, C., & Teddlie, C. (2009). *Foundations of mixed methods research: Integrating quantitative and qualitative approaches in the social and behavioral sciences.* SAGE.

Taylor, S. J., Bogdan, R., & DeVault, M. L. (2015). *Introduction to qualitative research methods: A guidebook and resource* (4th ed.). Wiley.

Timulak, L. (2007). Identifying core categories of client identified impact of helpful events in psychotherapy—A qualitative meta-analysis. *Psychotherapy Research, 17*(3), 305–314. https://doi.org/10.1080/10503300600608116

Timulak, L., & Elliott, R. (2003). Empowerment events in process-experiential psychotherapy of depression: An exploratory qualitative analysis. *Psychotherapy Research, 13*(4), 443–460. https://doi.org/10.1093/ptr/kpg043

Timulak, L., & Elliott, R. (2019). Taking stock of descriptive-interpretative qualitative psychotherapy research: Issues and observations from the front line. *Counselling & Psychotherapy Research, 19*(1), 8–15. https://doi.org/10.1002/capr.12197

Timulak, L., & Lietaer, G. (2001). Moments of empowerment: A qualitative analysis of positively experienced episodes in brief person-centred counselling. *Counselling & Psychotherapy Research, 1*(1), 62–73. https://doi.org/10.1080/14733140112331385268

Timulak, L., McElvaney, J., Keogh, D., Martin, E., Clare, P., Chepukova, E., & Greenberg, L. S. (2017). Emotion-focused therapy for generalized anxiety disorder: An exploratory study. *Psychotherapy, 54*(4), 361–366. https://doi.org/10.1037/pst0000128

Tufford, L., & Newman, P. (2012). Bracketing in qualitative research. *Qualitative Social Work: Research and Practice, 11*(1), 80–96. https://doi.org/10.1177/1473325010368316

Vygotsky, L. S. (1978). *Mind in society: The development of higher psychological processes.* Harvard University Press.

Wertz, F. J. (1983). From everyday to psychological description: Analyzing the moments of a qualitative data analysis. *Journal of Phenomenological Psychology, 14*(1–2), 197–241. https://doi.org/10.1163/156916283X00108

Wertz, F. J. (1985). Methods and findings in the study of a complex life event: Being criminally victimized. In A. Giorgi (Ed.), *Phenomenology and psychological research* (pp. 155–216). Duquesne University Press.

Index

About the Authors

Robert Elliott, PhD, is a professor of counselling at the University of Strathclyde. He received his doctorate in clinical psychology from the University of California, Los Angeles, and is professor emeritus of psychology at the University of Toledo (Ohio). He has spent most of his career as a psychotherapy researcher trying out and inventing different research methods. He is coauthor of *Facilitating Emotional Change* (1993), *Learning Emotion-Focused Therapy* (2004), and *Research Methods in Clinical Psychology* (3rd ed., 2015), as well as more than 170 journal articles and book chapters. Dr. Elliott is past president of the Society for Psychotherapy Research and previously coedited the journals *Psychotherapy Research* and *Person-Centered & Experiential Psychotherapies*. He is a fellow in the American Psychological Association (APA) divisions of Clinical Psychology, Psychotherapy, and Humanistic Psychology. He has received the Distinguished Research Career Award of the Society for Psychotherapy Research and the Carl Rogers Award from the APA Division of Humanistic Psychology.

Ladislav Timulak, PhD, is an associate professor at Trinity College Dublin, Ireland. He is course director of the Doctorate in Counselling Psychology course. Dr. Timulak is involved in the training of counselling psychologists and various psychotherapy trainings in Ireland and internationally. He is both an academic and a practitioner. He is interested in research methodology and psychotherapy research, particularly the development of emotion-focused therapy. He is currently adapting this form of therapy as a transdiagnostic treatment for depression, anxiety, and related disorders. He has written six books, over 80 peer-reviewed papers, and various chapters in both his native language, Slovak, and English. His most recent books include *Transforming Emotional Pain in Psychotherapy: An Emotion-Focused Approach* (2015) and *Transforming Generalized Anxiety: An Emotion-Focused Approach* (2017). Dr. Timulak serves on various editorial boards, and in the past served as a coeditor of *Counselling Psychology Quarterly*.

About the Series Editors

Clara E. Hill, PhD, earned her doctorate at Southern Illinois University in 1974. She started her career in 1974 as an assistant professor in the Department of Psychology, University of Maryland, College Park, and is currently there as a professor.

She is the president-elect of the Society for the Advancement of Psychotherapy, and has been the president of the Society for Psychotherapy Research, the editor of the *Journal of Counseling Psychology*, and the editor of *Psychotherapy Research*.

Dr. Hill was awarded the Leona Tyler Award for Lifetime Achievement in Counseling Psychology from Division 17 (Society of Counseling Psychology) and the Distinguished Psychologist Award from Division 29 (Society for the Advancement of Psychotherapy) of the American Psychological Association, the Distinguished Research Career Award from the Society for Psychotherapy Research, and the Outstanding Lifetime Achievement Award from the Section on Counseling and Psychotherapy Process and Outcome Research of the Society for Counseling Psychology. Her major research interests are helping skills, psychotherapy process and outcome, training therapists, dream work, and qualitative research.

She has published more than 250 journal articles, 80 chapters in books, and 17 books (including *Therapist Techniques and Client Outcomes: Eight Cases of Brief Psychotherapy*; *Helping Skills: Facilitating Exploration, Insight, and Action*; and *Dream Work in Therapy: Facilitating Exploration, Insight, and Action*).

Sarah Knox, PhD, joined the faculty of Marquette University in 1999 and is a professor in the Department of Counselor Education and Counseling Psychology in the College of Education. She earned her doctorate at the University of Maryland and completed her predoctoral internship at The Ohio State University.

Dr. Knox's research has been published in a number of journals, including *The Counseling Psychologist, Counselling Psychology Quarterly, Journal of Counseling Psychology, Psychotherapy, Psychotherapy Research,* and *Training and Education in Professional Psychology.* Her publications focus on the psychotherapy process and relationship, supervision and training, and qualitative research. She has presented her research both nationally and internationally and has provided workshops on consensual qualitative research at both U.S. and international venues.

She currently serves as coeditor-in-chief of *Counselling Psychology Quarterly* and is also on the publication board of Division 29 (Society for the Advancement of Psychotherapy) of the American Psychological Association. Dr. Knox is a fellow of Division 17 (Society of Counseling Psychology) and Division 29 (Society for the Advancement of Psychotherapy) of the American Psychological Association.